I SOLD 22 HOMES IN ONE DAY

About the Author

Rory O'Rourke is Principal and Licensee, with his wife, Robyn, of O'Rourke Realty Investments in Perth, Western Australia. Born on 17 October 1945 in Dublin, Ireland he migrated with his family to Australia as a nine-year-old arriving in Perth on 10 January 1955 with his parents, Tom and Rosaleen O'Rourke; his brothers, Brian 11 and Tom 6; and his sister, Cathy 3. They settled on the coast at Waterman's Bay.

Rory has been active in the building and real estate industries for nearly forty years. Among many other achievements in real estate, he was the top Western Australian multilisting representative in both sales and listings for 1981.

He has lectured on the themes of this book in five states of Australia and both islands of New Zealand. He is a Life Member of Apex Australia (Hamersley Club).

Rory and Robyn have two adult sons, Dean and Jarrad. Dean is building manager of a major WA home builder and Jarrad, having joined the family business at the age of fifteen, is now Sales Manager of O'Rourke Realty Investments.

Also by Rory O'Rourke

BORN FREE – TAXED TO DEATH

Front Cover Story

Car 62, Telethon Trek Vehicle. A 1970 Pontiac Parisienne in iron ore country, Western Australia.

A former wedding car, the O'Rourkes, Chris Kerns (Compac Marketing) and Dale Alcock (Dale Alcock Homes), the major sponsors, felt it lacked a honeymoon suite, and so we added one!

We raised approximately $24,000 for Telethon last year and will be entering in the trek again in July this year and hoping to raise as much money again.

All contributions and sponsorship welcome.

I Sold 22 Homes in One Day

Thinking Outside the Square

By Rory J. O'Rourke
Australian Multi Listing Record Holder

Published by O'Rourke Publishing Pty Ltd
Perth, Western Australia

First published in Australia in 2002
by O'Rourke Publishing Pty Ltd

National Library of Australia
Cataloguing-in-Publication data

O'Rourke, Rory James
I sold 22 homes in one day.

ISBN 0 9580343 0 3.

1. Real estate investment – Taxation – Australia. I. Title. II. Title: I sold 22 homes in one day.

333.33220994

Typesetting and cover layout by Nutshell Books, Western Australia
Printed in Australia by Griffin Press

Disclaimer: No liability accepted.

R.J. O'Rourke and O'Rourke Publishing Pty Ltd A.C.N. 009 120 334 state that the advice and information provided is of a general nature and neither purports nor intends to be specific to any individual. It has been prepared without regard to any particular person's investment objectives, financial situation and particular needs.

Dedication

This book is dedicated to my wife, Robyn, my partner in life and in business and also my best friend. I cannot thank you enough for your support – letting me chase my dreams and aspirations throughout our 32 years of marriage.

To my parents Thomas Joseph O'Rourke and my late mother Rosaleen for having the foresight to bring their young children to Australia in 1955 to give us a better future, and for the example you set for us to follow.

To my children, Dean and Jarrad. For your huge support, while I get in and out of trouble, as I learned the secrets of creating wealth. A special thanks to Jarrad, for keeping our business "on the rails" while I have been playing author.

To my two gorgeous daughters in law, Tania and Anna, thanks for becoming part of our life.

To every one I have ever met – for sharing your knowledge with me.

To all of you that have taken the time to read this book, hopefully it will help you.

"Leave wisdom, as well as wealth, to your future generations".

He's Back

From the ashes of one of the biggest real estate disasters in Australia's history, Rory O'Rourke has emerged alive and well and doing what he does best – marketing real estate for investment.

'I'd had financial hiccups before,' says Rory, 'but never anything as dramatic as this one. Will I make mistakes in the future? Yes. Will I make the same mistakes? Definitely not.'

He was a casualty of the recession we had to have. What tipped him over the edge was a huge provisional tax bill. He tells the full story in this book.

People say he went bankrupt. Not true. He did a Part X, undertaking to pay out his creditors within 48 months. He managed it in less than half that time.

Before the debacle Rory O'Rourke was worth millions. Guess what. He's worth millions again.

Foreword

Real estate represents 100% of the world's wealth.

Negative gearing is the best form of positive gearing.

Tax minimisation is the secret of wealthy.

How do they do it? Through Real Estate Investment!

Real Estate Investment brings you a double benefit. It enables you to accrue Capital Wealth, and if structured properly it can reduce your tax. In fact it can eradicate your personal tax and start building tax credits.

"One good real estate investment is worth a lifetime of toil" *Henry Ford*

The future of Real Estate is in selling properties for investment.

My best day, for number of sales, was 6 February 1982. I sold 22 homes in one day.

Rory J. O'Rourke

Contents

Preface

During the late 1980s and early 1990s I conducted many seminars for The Professionals real estate group in five states of Australia and both islands of New Zealand. On hundreds of occasions I was asked by participants if I could recommend an advanced text on real estate investment, in particular on the marketing of residential property for investment.

I had to say that, sadly, there was nothing: all the books and educational aids I knew of were targeted at the novice coming into the industry, with heavy emphasis on listing and selling to owner-occupiers.

It has taken me a while, but I am now pleased to offer this contribution to the literature on real estate marketing, with the hope that it goes at least a good part of the way towards filling the gap.

The future of real estate is in the investment market. We all need to be proactive, not reactive, in meeting the challenges ahead.

Rory J. O'Rourke

Frequently Asked Questions

Here are a few of the most common questions I have been asked about investing in real estate:

What is gearing?

Gearing is controlling a large investment with a small amount of money.

What is positive gearing?

Positive gearing is when the rent is greater than the expenses, so a profit is added to the top of your normal income.

What is negative gearing?

When the outgoings on your investment property – i.e. mortgage interest, rates, taxes etc. – exceed your rental income, you create a negative income on this property. This is deductible from your other income, thus reducing your tax. You can also claim the borrowing costs, the depreciation on the building since 1985 and the depreciation on the chattels. These are deductions, not expenses, thus reducing your taxable income further.

What is meant by equity borrowings?

If you currently own a property valued at $100,000 on which you have a $20,000 mortgage, you have equity of $80,000. You can use this $80,000 equity as security to borrow against. These borrowings may be used to assist in purchasing investment property. Interest on these equity borrowings is tax deductible under these circumstances.

What does shortfall mean?

Shortfall is the difference between all outgoings on a property and the rent received – the actual cash deficiency after all other legal deductions.

What is a capital gain?

If you have a $100,000 investment property that increases 15 per cent in value, your capital gain is $15,000. It should be noted however that, as an investor who is negatively geared, you might have placed a deposit of only $15,000 on your investment. Your return on your deposit would then be 100 per cent. There is **no capital gains tax** to pay unless you sell the property.

What is capital gains tax?

If the owner of a property, having held it for at least a year, sells it for more than they paid for it, half of the CAPITAL GAIN is added to the seller's income for that year in assessing tax liability.

How long should I hold an investment property?

It is advisable to hold an investment property as long as possible. Purchase costs and selling costs are considerable, and it is therefore unwise to consider investing short term. Property values double approximately every eight years, and you should consider holding a property at least for that length of time to maximise your capital wealth gains.

What is a 'buffer' and how does it work?

A buffer is created by earmarking a certain amount of 'excess' money, normally obtained from EQUITY BORROWINGS. These funds are used to assist in paying interest on the borrowings and SHORTFALLS on the investment property. I recommend that tax refunds created by NEGATIVE GEARING are also placed into the buffer. It is advisable to establish a buffer fund substantial enough to assist with paying all outgoings on the investment property for a period of approximately eighteen months. The buffer fund is also a security blanket. It is advisable that you contribute personal savings to it whenever you are able to. This will extend its life span and give it the capacity to cope with any unforeseeable developments, e.g. rises in interest rates, maintenance costs, vacancies etc.

Why not create a buffer fund that will last longer than eighteen months? Why not three years? Or five years?

As you are likely to create your BUFFER fund from EQUITY BORROWINGS, and you have to pay interest on those borrowings, why borrow more than you have to initially? It is far more economical to remove further equity borrowings in eighteen months' time than to pay interest on a larger amount from day one.

What happens in eighteen months' time if my buffer runs out?

Eighteen months from the time of your investment purchase, its value will have risen along with the value of your other property, so you have new equity borrowing power.

You can remove some of this newfound equity to purchase more property and prepay interest on it, as well as to replenish the buffer.

How do I choose an investment property?

It is important to detach your emotions in regard to investment purchases. You are not purchasing a property you would like to live in; you are purchasing tax deductibility and capital wealth by way of bricks and mortar. A tenant will live in it. Any property can provide you with a tax deduction, but it is important that you also maximise your **capital wealth**. The location of your investment is the single most important consideration. You should listen to our advice in this regard. We go out to manage your portfolio. If the property is not let, neither party makes any money, and if we can't make it work for you, why would you buy any more from us? If you live in another State, these remarks still apply. We have many clients outside Western Australia.

How do I know that the investment is worth what I am paying for it?

As an investor you are likely to invest only 15 per cent in the property. Because a lender is going to put in 85 per cent of the funds, they will insist that a licensed valuer puts a figure on the property. If it does not come up to valuation, they will not be prepared to lend 85 per cent of the price. There would therefore be no point in us attempting to sell you an investment property for more than its market value.

What is going to happen to interest rates?

Interest rates always have and always will fluctuate, depending on the economic policies and pressures of the day. For investors in real estate any interest rate increase is softened, as it directly increases tax deductibility. If you hold a property for the suggested eight-year minimum, it is likely you will see a substantial variance in rates over that period. Rents will also increase to offset the interest hike. All costs are passed on to the consumer (tenants).

Why should I take out an interest-only loan?

The interest is fully tax deductible, whereas any amount paid off the principal is never tax deductible.

What's in it for me?

Currently the tax you pay is lost forever. By negative gearing, your tax liability can be reduced or eliminated. This tax saving is used to help pay the holding costs of your investment. History proves that the value of real estate property goes up. The longer you hold your investment, the more your capital wealth grows.

What happens if I have a problem or need advice after I have purchased an investment?

O'Rourke Realty Investments provides full 'after sales' service. Any advice or assistance that you require will be given, and regular liaison is maintained with clients. It is imperative that your personal situation in regard to income, equity availability etc. be reviewed regularly. When our company manages your investment property, we advise you in regard to rent increases, property values and so on. It is important that you trust our advice. For our part, we are conscious that we earn trust only by providing a reliable, professional service.

What if I get the tenant from hell?

Hopefully you have Landlord Protection Insurance, for $150 per year, it's the best insurance to cover that rogue tenant damage and will cover you for loss of rent up to 15 weeks.

What are the Property Management charges if the property is vacant?

NIL

Can I reduce this year's tax?

Most definitely. You can pre pay next years interest, up to a maximum of 13 months.

Who pays us?

Fortunately the vendor pays us commission on each sale we make. Secondly all landlords pay us for our property management, hopefully you will become a landlord also.

What is the greatest hazard inherent in real estate investments?

"Expert" friends, bad advice or no advice at all. Real estate investment is a highly specialized field, and requires up to the minute knowledge. The expert advice is available from O'Rourke Realty Investments. We specialize in investment properties and property management, and our knowledge and experience will put you on the right track – and keep you there.

Do you think that everyone should invest in Real Estate?

No. Each type of investment enjoys it's own advantages and benefits. You must have some savings or an equity facility for that rainy day. It's up to you.

Introduction

Two events in my life each played a big part in changing my thinking about the business of real estate.

The first was a journey to Scotland that my wife and I undertook in 1979 as representatives of Apex Australia. As I explain in later pages, what we saw and heard there set off a train of thought that in the end had me realising home ownership was a vanishing option for most Australians, just as it was for people in other parts of the world. As I thought about this, it hit me that over the past century there had been an immense shift in how home purchases were financed in this country – from our grandparents having to pay cash to the new generation actually being paid to become home owners. Where could this process possibly end?

If home ownership was becoming an impossible dream for most people, who would supply their housing? The Government? For various reasons, no. It would have to be private investors.

Home ownership had defined the middle class, so it seemed the middle class was actually disappearing. If that was the case, it would leave only the rich and the poor. Which would I be? As I was born in Ireland, God didn't give me a brain, so I tossed a coin. Fortunately it came up rich.

My journey to riches hasn't been a smooth one, which brings me to the second of those events that shaped my thinking. About ten years ago the Taxation Office, aided and abetted by a bank, very nearly dragged me under, which made me think more deeply about taxation than I ever had before. Pretty soon I realised that taxation was in fact the biggest expense most people face throughout their lives, and was a real hindrance to their prosperity unless they did something about it.

This will give you some idea where I was coming from when I set out to write this book. All the themes I've touched on above are explored fully in the pages that follow.

1

Professional Salespeople

Who are the highest paid people in the world? Some of the highest paid are salespeople – yes, top salespeople earn more than most professionals. Sadly 20 per cent do 80 per cent of the business and 80 per cent do the other 20 per cent. How do you move from one group to the other? By being creative and by being different.

I believe I still hold the daily, weekly and monthly multilisting Australian records since 1980, namely eighteen in a day, thirty-six in a week and forty-eight in a month. That same year I listed 123 multilisted properties in six months and sold 110 such properties in the same six months. These figures do not include properties that were not multilisted. **How did I do it?** *Read on.*

Who are My Clients?

Thirty-five years ago I would wake up and think someone in Australia will buy real estate today. All I had to do was find him/her. But I found I was competing against every other agent in Australia looking for the same person.

Today I wake up and think someone will pay tax today. All I have to do is find him/her. Who have you ever met who wants to pay more tax? More to the point, are there any people you know who would like to reduce their tax?

Manage Your Business

Everybody is in business, it's just the majority of the population don't realise it.

Everyday you manage the household budget. You work out what you can afford to spend after you have paid the mortgage, rates, school fees etc. Anything you have left over is your 'profit' – you manage your cash flow. The essence of all businesses is cash flow management. The major difference between you as an individual and a business is you pay your expenses out of what's left of your income having paid tax. A business pays all expenses and then only pays tax on profits. Buying a real estate investment allows you to operate as a business.

1

We all should have 'a business strategy' the following is the one I use, more complicated than you may need, but the principles are the same.

No matter what business your in:

It costs ten times as much to gain a new client, as it does to keep an existing client happy.

How much time do we put into keeping existing clients satisfied, too often very little.

Even in Real Estate, you generally saw the client, making a large investment, buying an investment property.

Will their new property purchase go up? **Yes**

Will their own home still go up? **Yes**

Will their personal income go up? **Yes**

Will their personal taxable income go up also over time? **Yes**

If you could show them how they could further reduce their tax whilst increasing their wealth, would they be any better off.

Everyone is a candidate to buy Real Estate from me.

Most Real Estate agents see their rent role as future sales!!

I see our rent role as future purchasers.

In this following illustration I start at the bottom rung of the ladder:

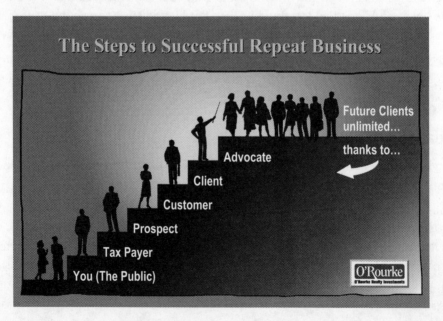

1. *You (the public)!!*
   What do you all do? Pay tax! Is it a good investment??

2. *So you are all tax payers!!*
   What return did you see for last years contribution?? Did you get a letter of thanks from Canberra.

3. *Prospect!*
   What prospect? Would you be any better off if you could reduce your tax, even eradicate your tax?? **Yes**

4. *Customer!!*
   If I can reduce your tax by buying Real Estate, if you had paid $24,000 in tax last year and you put the similar $24,000 this year into interest i.e $400,000 @ 6% interest = $24,000 you would have additional capital growth say of 10% on $400,000 equals $40,000. Your wealth just grew by $40,000, what did you say you gained from last year's donation of $24,000.

5. *Client??*
   Satisfied clients is what all businesses should be out to achieve. Why? Satisfied clients create "advocates".

6. *Advocates!!*
   When your clients start recommending their friends, their relatives, their neighbours to you "your future clients are unlimited".

7. ***Your future clients are unlimited.***

We all need to put more time into our existing client base. The rest will automatically follow.

We all know that word of mouth is the best sort of advertising.

All businesses share the same recipe for success. A sound business strategy coupled with sound financial management.

Finding a Salesperson

What attributes do I look for in a salesperson?

- ethics, background, family, values
- the fire in the belly
- the desire for knowledge
- the desire to improve.

The Real Estate Institute

The Real Estate Institute of Australia and its state branches have done an excellent job in Australia. I have been a proud member of the Real Estate Institute of Western Australia and its Multiple Listing Service for the past twenty-three years. I cannot speak highly enough of the standards this body sets for practising real estate agents.

The industry has come a long way in the public's perception thanks to the tireless efforts of the state presidents, the committees and of course the executive directors and staffs of the state bodies – plus all the practising real estate agents who give up their time to make a professional industry for everyone.

The Supervisory Boards of Real Estate and Business Agents in each state have also been setting the highest goals for our industry, and the state technical education departments, along with the institutes, are doing a great job in furthering higher education for sales representatives. In Western Australia now a sales representative must spend four weeks in training – three in the classroom, with rigorous training each day and homework at night, and one at the sponsor firm's office. The applicant must also find approximately $950 in fees and obtain a police clearance certificate prior to being able to commence as a Licensed Sales Representative.

Multilisting

Two principals of Mal Dempsey & Associates found themselves in an unusual situation when Mr Mal Dempsey (left), as Chairman of the Multiple Listing Service, presented to his partner, Mr Rory J. O'Rourke, the MLS's service sales championship shield. Mr O'Rourke was the 1981 top selling and listing representative of the MLS. The enormous growth of the company over the past two years was highlighted by the fact that it finished second for properties sold through the MLS. This was an extraordinary achievement considering that the company operates from only one branch in WA compared with the winning company, which has nine branches.

The Multiple Listing Service is the benchmark for all the institute's members. It is the only accredited source of sales evidence that we and our peers are judged on. As you would know, the figures are released each month and then carried forward to the end of the year. Monthly winners in both listings and sales are noted for the individual representative and the individual office.

These monthly figures are probably one of the best tools that an agent can use with a vendor who is thinking of listing a property. Sadly, salespeople are not always believed, but showing a client how you fared the previous month or the previous year proves your performance.

The Real Estate Institute of Western Australia Incorporated
Established 1918

31st August, 1981.

R. O'Rourke,
Mal Dempsey & Associates,
95 Scarborough Beach Road,
SCARBOROUGH, W.A., 6019.

Dear Rory,

The Chairman; and members of the Multiple Listing Service Committee take great pleasure in congratulating you on becoming both Top Selling Rep and Top Listing Rep (by number of listings sold) for 1980/81. Also for becoming a member of the Million Dollar Club.

Your presence is requested at the M.L.S. Annual Prize Night to be held on Friday 2nd October, 1981 at Subiaco Football Club, starting at 7 p.m..
Enclosed are two complimentary tickets. We look forward to sharing the evening with youself and your wife.

Yours sincerely,

KATE A FEARNALL
for R J OCKERBY

REIWA letter confirming top sales
and listing ranking

Talk is cheap. Our ethics must be second to none if we are going to last in this or any other industry. The client must be *number one* – not just at the point of listing but also from that minute onwards. I have found that looking after your clients properly creates more and more sales.

Thanks to the multilisting system I can claim, without any room for dispute, the sales figures I quoted earlier. I have also won dozens of multilisting monthly awards for both sales and listings, and in one year won both the sales and listing awards for WA.

Spreading the Message

We must all continue to strive to lift our industry to a higher plateau. For my own part, while I try to learn something new every day, I also now see myself as an educator. As it appears to me, these two aspects go together. One of the things I do is conduct a public seminar every week. We all need to share our knowledge with each other and with the public. The following letters on pages 7 and 8 from a client sums up what I am talking about.
I sold him fifteen properties and he started with only $10,000. He is still a client today.

Gerry Harlock, had bought eight properties from me prior to moving into one himself.

Did all the seven properties go up? Yes. All the expenses were tax deductible other than the rent he was paying. He was working on a two week on – two week off roster then five weeks in Libya and two weeks off. Why have your property sitting vacant for two to five weeks at time?

Gerry was initially renting with four other men in Hamersley, Western Australia. When he was away at work someone else was home and so on.

In 1984 Gerry Harlock Wrote...

1st. October 84,

Dear Rory,

Just a few lines hoping all is well with you. I've spent the last couple of nights trying to put my affairs in order and update them after starting with the taxman I thought I'd carry on.

As I sorted things out and they fell into order I gradually came up with a portfolio that is quite impressive. I never really realised until now how much you have really done to help me. Because without that help I would definitely not be where I am today, it is all due to the interest you have taken in me. I know I've been a bit slow to catch on at times this is partly the reason it's taken me so long to get around to this.

I don't know if I have really thanked you properly in the past and incase I forget at times in the future I want you to know that I thank you sincerely for all your help and advice (I am gradually learning from you) Your being a friend as well is something I don't take lightly. I've written this because verbally I may not say all that I want to because of embarrassment. So once again Rory thanks for everything

Regards

Gerry Harlock.

7

By 2002 Gerry Harlock has the Benefit of Hindsight

2nd January 2002

O'Rourke Realty Investments
62,Scarborough Beach Rd
Scarborough
WA 6019

Dear Rory,

It's now 2002 and eighteen years since we first met in Derby. This was the time when I embarked nervously on the path to buying fifteen odd properties through you. Hindsight has seen what good advise you gave me.

Your advise is still second to none.

All the best for the New Year

Kind Regards

Gerry Harlock

Gerry Harlock

2

Why Don't Real Estate Agents Own Real Estate?

Why don't real estate agents own real estate? Most of them own one house and two cars. Obviously cars are a better investment than real estate?

Why doesn't every real estate agent own a number of properties? Is it perhaps that every property they ever sold went down in value?

Recently an ex-employee of mine from twenty years ago bought two properties from me. He told me the reason he was doing it was to 'shut my mouth'. What he was referring to was that every time I saw him I would ask him the question at the head of this chapter. Thanks, I appreciated the business. And perhaps he's beginning to see the point.

New Directions

What are each of you doing? Are you still operating in the same manner as real estate salespeople have done for the last thirty years? Fortunately we are all individuals: we all think differently, and what suits me won't necessarily suit you. But I believe our industry needs to move decisively in a new direction.

I have learned a lot in the fifty-six years of my life. Like most of you I have, during that time, tried different methods in whatever job I was doing. I commenced work as a costing clerk with a large building company while I was studying accountancy, but I have always found myself drawn towards marketing and selling generally, irrespective of the field. To me, marketing is an integral part of selling. The word 'marketing' is especially true with real estate because a two-fold sell is involved.

- Your marketing presentation can mean the difference between getting the listing and not getting it. In real estate this is the all-important sale – without the listing, your phone doesn't ring. Many of us underestimate the time needed to get that listing. The vendor needs to be sold; he needs to know you are the best in the business. If you don't believe it, you have no chance of convincing him. Your marketing presentation needs to be second to none.

- We only get paid when we sell the property.

The Growing Market

But when we set out to make the sale, are we just looking for someone who wants to buy themselves a place to live? If so, we are ignoring a huge and growing part of the market – the residential investment market. Could it be the case that we're not seeing the wood for the trees?

Allowing a certain period of time, say three to five years, every property we have ever sold has gone up in value. And gone up faster than the rate of inflation. Is your experience any different?

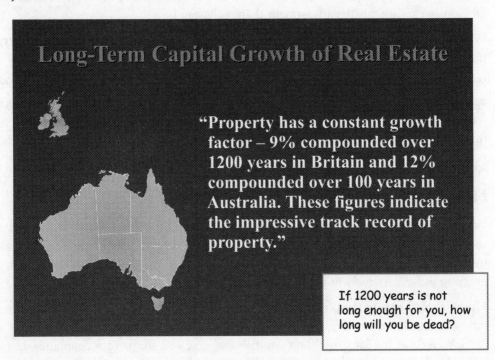

Long-Term Capital Growth of Real Estate

"Property has a constant growth factor – 9% compounded over 1200 years in Britain and 12% compounded over 100 years in Australia. These figures indicate the impressive track record of property."

If 1200 years is not long enough for you, how long will you be dead?

All real estate agents should be leading by example. If you don't believe in real estate, what chance does the public have of seeing the opportunities?

Yes, why aren't you buying real estate? If you structure the deals sensibly, it need not cost you any money. The tax you used to pay can now be converted into interest repayments while your investment property increases in value. If you were to prepay next year's interest in advance, this would reduce your current year's tax substantially.

Saving Tax by Buying Property

The following example will illustrate the point. If you prepaid $60,000 in interest on a property investment, and your income was $130,000, then, ignoring all the other deductions you might have, your new taxable income would be reduced accordingly:

Income	$130,000
Less prepayment	$ 60,000
New taxable income	$ 70,000

In this tax bracket you would be saving tax of 47 per cent, which is approximately $28,000 in this case.

Do you see where I'm coming from?

3

The Changing Face of Residential Real Estate

Are you keeping up with the changes? The future of residential real estate is the investment market. The rental market is surely going to expand.

Our grandparents paid cash for a property. Our parents put 50 per cent deposit and borrowed the other 50 per cent from a bank over a period of seven to ten years with a principal-and-interest loan. We begged, borrowed and stole to come up with a 20 per cent deposit, and borrowed the other 80 per cent from a bank over twenty years or a building society over thirty years on a principal-and-interest basis. For the first five to seven years we weren't paying anything off the principal (even though the loan was called 'principal-and-interest').

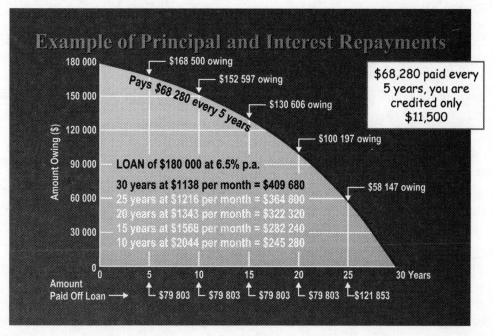

Example of Principal and Interest Repayments

180 000 — $168 500 owing

Pays $68 280 every 5 years

$152 597 owing

$130 606 owing

$68,280 paid every 5 years, you are credited only $11,500

$100 197 owing

LOAN of $180 000 at 6.5% p.a.

30 years at $1138 per month = $409 680

25 years at $1216 per month = $364 800

20 years at $1343 per month = $322 320

15 years at $1568 per month = $282 240

10 years at $2044 per month = $245 280

$58 147 owing

Amount Owing ($)

Amount Paid Off Loan → $79 803 $79 803 $79 803 $79 803 $121 853

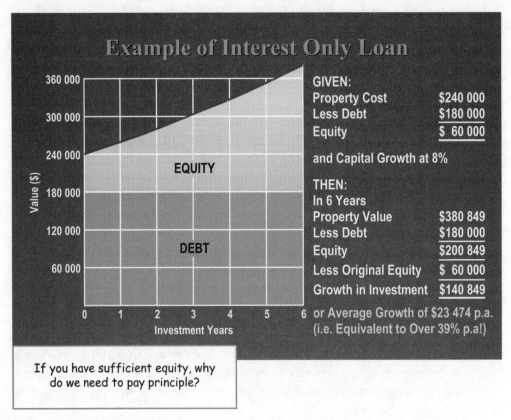

Example of Interest Only Loan

GIVEN:
Property Cost	$240 000
Less Debt	$180 000
Equity	$ 60 000

and Capital Growth at 8%

THEN:
In 6 Years
Property Value	$380 849
Less Debt	$180 000
Equity	$200 849
Less Original Equity	$ 60 000
Growth in Investment	$140 849

or Average Growth of $23 474 p.a.
(i.e. Equivalent to Over 39% p.a!)

If you have sufficient equity, why do we need to pay principle?

Diminishing Inputs

Our children took out Key Start loans. That was on the basis of 5 per cent deposit. In their case, borrowing 95 per cent over thirty years, the first principal payment would be in the vicinity of six to nine years away, depending on the interest rate. Key Start then dropped the minimum deposit to 2 per cent, with no mortgage insurance. In the new millennium the Commonwealth Government began offering a $7,000 gift on established homes and a $14,000 gift on new homes for first-home owners, including new immigrants, plus up to $2,000 government assistance towards their legal costs. Their 'deposits' became in effect minus $7,000 and minus $14,000. This was flagged as a temporary arrangement, but we were not far into 2001/02 when the Prime Minister announced that the grants would be extended to 30 June 2002, though in the case of new homes the amount would be reduced to $10,000.

The Future?

So in my lifetime I have seen my grandparents paying cash and people my children's age being given $7,000 and $14,000 grants. (Who really pays this money? The taxpayer.

Who is that? You and me.) Where do we go from here? Will the Government convert title to leasehold instead of freehold? Will we go the Japanese way of heirloom mortgages? These are taken over a hundred years, so you commit your great-grandson/daughter to debts of many millions of yen, equivalent to millions of Australian dollars, before they are even thought about.

It is up to us to educate the public and encourage their accountants to show them how to reduce their tax while increasing their wealth. Become proactive rather than reactive. Position yourself such that you **bequeath wisdom, along with your money, so that the fourteenth and fifteenth generations after you can benefit from your hard-earning life. And pass this wisdom on to your clients also**.

4

Investment Technology in the 21st Century

'Technology' – could that be the right word here? Technology means 'gathering all available learning and technical skills and implementing them in the best practical way to achieve a goal'. So yes, it does apply.

There are a lot of books around on the normal approach to the day-to-day running of a real estate office; but what about the changes, the new directions, the whole new market that you can benefit from?

Being Creative

I have been in the building and real estate industry for thirty-nine years. For the last twenty-two of these I have been waking up in the morning believing I needed to be different and to be creative; for the previous seventeen I had basically gone along with the process that most of us humans are involved in. I sold a reasonable amount of property, I renovated property and I tried different methods of marketing. I actually believed the creed we had all been taught: 'It's risky to borrow money'. I even thought it would be nice to win the lottery. **I have since found that we win the lottery daily, weekly, monthly and yearly if we own real estate**.

Here is the first basic point about investing in real estate: it is important to own a minimum of two properties. While you only own one property, every other one is going up at the same rate – similar to similar. Once you own two, you truly benefit.

If we look at our friends – our upwardly mobile home-owning friends – the best we can hope to do is sell them a property every six to seven years; yet so often one member or other of a married couple has already seen a property before they contact us, and simply wants our advice on whether it is a good buy. We, as a good friend, give the property the 'thumbs up' – unless we think it is seriously overvalued. These sales are a very emotive exercise. What they are looking for is their dream home, and they both have to like it.

What is a Good Investment Property?

With an investment property they do not need to like it. The only questions that require answers are:

- Will it go up in value over time?
- Am I happy to manage it?
- Will it give the tax relief they require?

On the matter of tax, if you have a choice between paying 17 per cent to 47 per cent tax and paying 6 per cent to 7.5 per cent interest, and if the interest is deductible and the tax is not, which would you rather pay? Hopefully you came up with the 7.5 per cent interest as your answer. What do you know about tax? Read on...and subscribe to CCH.

As early as 1984 the industry recognised my expertise in Investment Realty.

ROY WESTON real estate

PROPERTY INVESTOR

A publication of the Roy Weston Real Estate Group.   No. 2   OCTOBER '84

Head Office Building, 4 Thelma Street, West Perth.

Investment Technology in the 80's

by Rory J. O'Rourke
Commissioner for Declarations

About the author:

He is co-principal of the real estate firm, Mal Dempsey Rory O'Rourke, with 15 years in the building and real estate industry, and is one of the top investment real estate consultants in Australia. He is a life member of the Million Dollar Club of the Multiple Listing Service (a division of R.E.I.W.A.) and has set records as the top listing and top selling representative for that organisation. He is married, with two boys.

Rory O'Rourke was interviewed by the editor of the Roy Weston Property Investor and gave these frank answers, which explain why he has assisted more than three hundred Eastern States clients to purchase residential and commercial investment properties in Perth.

Q: What do you mean by investment technology?
A: *Technology is the nation's lifeline; it is a word which rolls easily off the tongue. To me it means gathering all the available real estate learning and technical skills at my disposal and implementing them in the best practical way to show my clients not only why they should invest in real estate but why they cannot afford not to invest in real estate!*

Q: Does that mean a polished marketing presentation?

A: *To me, marketing is a very intricate part of selling. Your marketing presentation when listing a property, means the difference between getting the listing or not. Again, we only get paid when we sell the property and so marketing is again of the utmost importance.*

Q: Does your marketing strategy differ from other real estate salespeople?

A: *It certainly does. The majority of agents are looking for people who want to buy real estate; I am looking for people who pay too much tax and believe me, I have never found a person who doesn't pay enough! Everyone is a prospect for my gearing exercises.*

Q: What do you mean by GEARING?

A: *By gearing, I mean controlling a large investment with a small amount of money. This is done by borrowing or mortgaging. The property owner, and not the man who holds the mortgage, stands to gain in a rising market. For example, if A and B own identical buildings worth $60,000 each, A had a clear title while B has a $40,000 mortgage. If the value of each building increases by one third, A has increased his equity by one third from $60,000 to $80,000. But B's equity has soared up 100 per cent from $20,000 to $40,000.*

Q: Are there any other benefits?

A: *The real benefit is yet to come — A has to pay tax on his income as he only has minimum deductions, that is rates, land tax, management fees, etc. While*

The Directors

ROY WESTON REAL ESTATE

4 Thelma Street, West Perth
Post Office Box 728, West Perth 6005
Telephone: 322 7222

October 16, 1984.

Mr. R. J. O'Rourke,
Co-Principal,
Mal Dempsey Rory O'Rourke Real Estate,
95 Scarborough Beach Road,
SCARBOROUGH,   6019.

Dear Rory,

Herewith are a few copies of our Property Investor Newsletter for October 1984. We printed 11,000 copies of this edition, of which 6,000 copies approximately were distributed through the Perth Chamber of Commerce newspaper.

Your article has pride of place on the front page and we would like to sincerely thank you for allowing us to feature it in our publication.

Yours sincerely,

DEREK PARK,
CHAIRMAN OF DIRECTORS.

Encs.

Directors
Derek C. Park F.R.E.I., Brian J. Newman A.A.I.V., Stuart W. Weston Bus. (W.A.I.T.)

Computers

Computer technology has changed our lives for ever. We all have computers...

Palm held

Laptop

Desktop

We all use a variety of software packages, we have two exclusive programmes for the Real Estate professional.

Bank Qualification

Investment Analyser

We all use computers for communication at work and at home:

> Palmheld computers, giving a property reporting system integrated with the office property management software. Easier and much more efficient.

The web

Email

Text messages

Web Site

Samples of pages from our innovative web site follow, go to **www.orourke.com.au** for the complete picture.

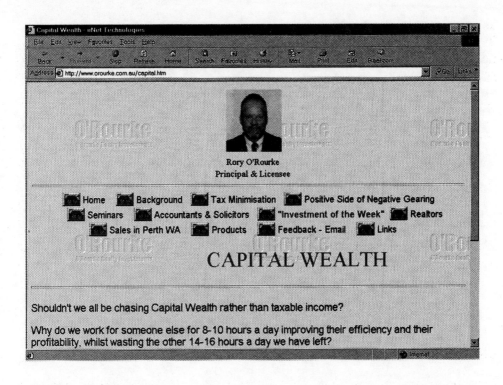

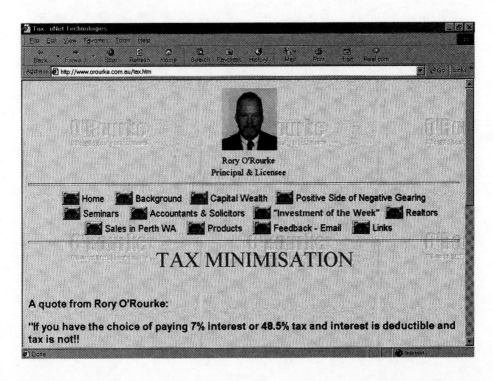

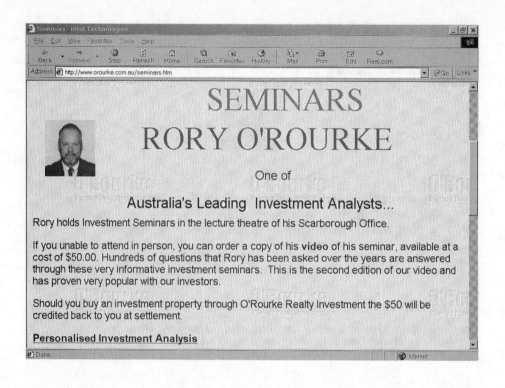

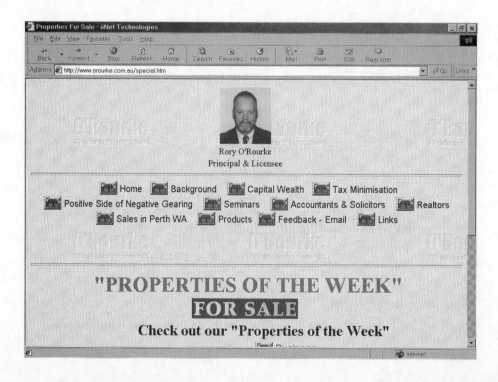

5

Every Real Estate Office Needs an Investment Analyst

'Thinking Outside the Square'

It is my contention that an investment analyst/coordinator is needed in every real estate office today. Change is slow in coming to our industry, but any of us can leap ahead of the pack by having someone in our office concentrating on the huge untouched investment market that is out there.

An investment coordinator in a real estate office fills much the same function as a financial controller in a car dealership. The financial controller has brought big changes to motor vehicle industry sales departments – and all other areas of the business – and most car dealerships today make as much profit out of the financing of purchases as from actual sales. The financial controller is a professional with specialised knowledge of all avenues of finance and the various aspects of leasing, which ensures that most deals go through smoothly and so makes for a more efficient operation.

What an Investment Coordinator can Contribute

In a real estate office the work of the investment coordinator has bearing on the activities of both the sales and property management departments. He or she might or might not be directly involved in sales, but one thing they should definitely be involved in is continual reassessment of existing clients in terms of their equity status and hence their capacity to purchase more property without having to find additional cash. Another aspect is taking account of how increases in rents could have shifted a property from negative to positive gearing, and being ready to propose restructuring and further purchases to bring the portfolio back into a negative gearing situation – at the same time, of course, adding to the client's capital wealth. Positive gearing refers of course to the situation where income from a property exceeds the interest payments and other expenses, such as rates, insurance, maintenance and management fees. The surplus is added to the owner's income and subject to income tax.

A further difference from the car dealership is that, whereas the financial controller there is basically concerned with organising finance for a particular item that the customer wants to purchase, his counterpart in the real estate agency will explore a whole range of possibilities with a client. Purchasers might be advised that they could buy as many as five properties rather than pay cash for one, or that a duplex site offers the possibility of renovating the existing home while building a second at the rear. They can be shown how to restructure their existing financial obligations and consolidate them into one loan, thus reducing their monthly repayments. Those selling property can be shown how to help a sale by offering vendor's terms.

The investment coordinator can also assist sales staff by determining the best marketing avenues, keeping them aware of alternative financing possibilities and putting tax packages together for all their listings. Ultimately their role in relation to real estate sales is taking a minority market and converting it into a majority market.

In the area of property management the investment coordinator can advise how, an upgrade of a particular property would more than pay for itself in terms of the higher rental the home would then attract. It can also be this person's job to make discreet inquiries about other properties owned by a client, and by other members of the client's family, with the aim of bringing them into management. This would in turn create the opportunity for proposing use of equity to buy additional real estate.

It costs ten times as much to find a new client as it does to re-assess existing clients and sell them additional properties. By and large sales and property management departments don't have the time to do this, but it can be a core responsibility of this specialised member of staff.

One way we have of attracting new clients is by conducting weekly investment seminars, and we have had such success with them that I can thoroughly recommend the approach. Your investment coordinator could make an important contribution to the running of such seminars.

Coordinating Finance

The investment coordinator can act as a liaison officer coordinating all the facets of finance. They need to become fully conversant with all aspects, the various benefits available to a landlord and depreciation – both building and chattels. They must know all the deductible items versus the capitalised items, understand positive gearing versus negative gearing, and combine all their knowledge with marketing ability. Most important, they must know the tax law and keep abreast of changes in it by studying the CCH updates, of which more later. And they must be very familiar with the VTDI form – about this too I'll have more to say.

This member of your team could also be a licensed finance broker, enabling the finance to be set in-house. This would add another very profitable department to the business. Some real estate firms have set up separate companies to carry out this service, for example Ray White Financial Services.

Finding the Right Person

The position of investment coordinator is not an easy one to fill. I would prefer to get hold of a good marketer with basic knowledge of the tax and finance sides rather than employ an accountant, or any other analytical-type person, and attempt to train them to become a marketer. Finance can be learnt, and there are excellent computer programs available that can help the marketer overcome any lack of tax knowledge, but it is very hard to change the rigid mindset of a lot of accountants.

A good marketer must be creative and willing to be different. The watchword is: EXPERIMENT, EXPERIMENT, EXPERIMENT. If one method doesn't work, try another.

Tools of the Trade – "Investment Analyser" Software

Having the right props and tools is important. Among the things I call 'props' are photographs and other material about previous successful projects, which I show to a client when I want to recommend a similar development.

Among the major tools these days are computer programs, especially one that deals with negative gearing. A new financial coordinator might be given an exercise on two blocks of cheap units, a computer analysis being done on each to show how much a person needs to find if purchasing one, two, three or four units. This software is now available for laptops as well as office computers, and so all questions can be answered in the client's own home or on site – even on the bonnet of a car! The O'Rourke Investment Analyser program is comprehensive, user-friendly and client focused as can be seen from the following screen captures on pages 26 to 29.

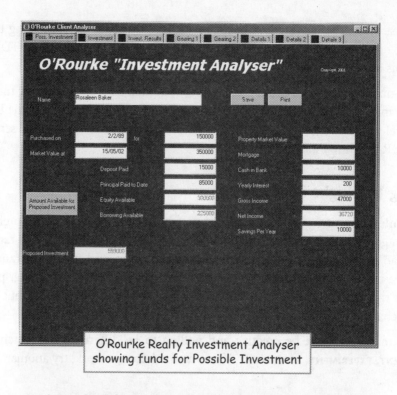

O'Rourke Realty Investment Analyser
showing funds for Possible Investment

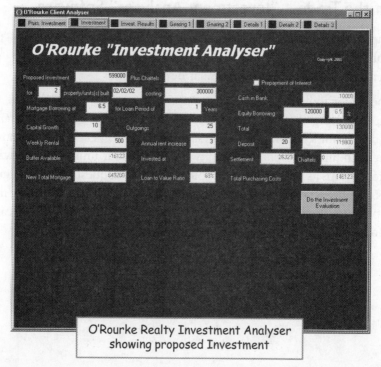

O'Rourke Realty Investment Analyser
showing proposed Investment

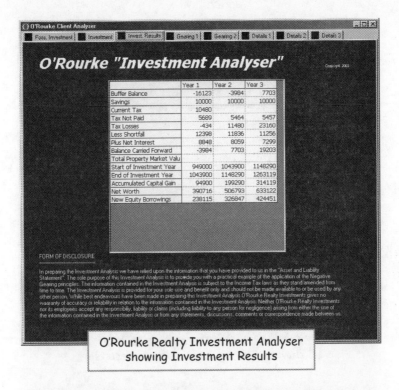

O'Rourke Realty Investment Analyser
showing Investment Results

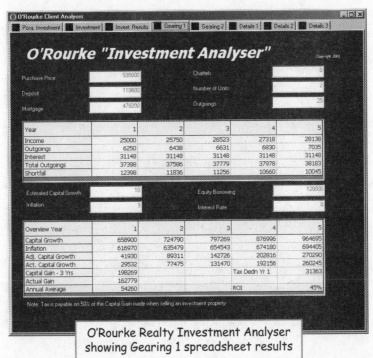

O'Rourke Realty Investment Analyser
showing Gearing 1 spreadsheet results

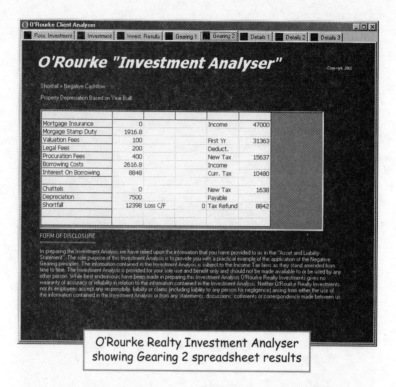

O'Rourke Realty Investment Analyser
showing Gearing 2 spreadsheet results

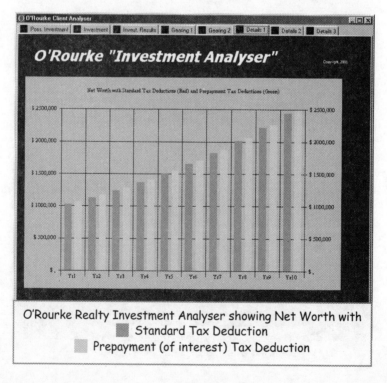

O'Rourke Realty Investment Analyser showing Net Worth with
Standard Tax Deduction
Prepayment (of interest) Tax Deduction

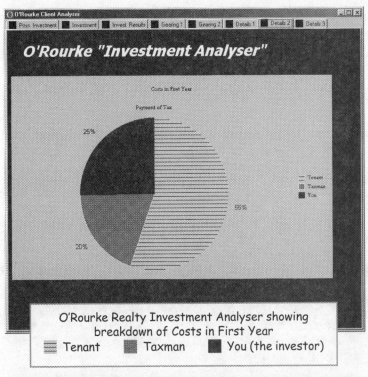

O'Rourke Realty Investment Analyser showing
breakdown of Costs in First Year
Tenant   Taxman   You (the investor)

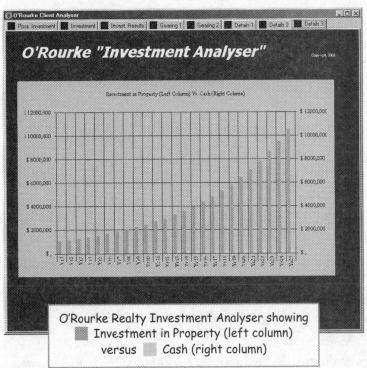

O'Rourke Realty Investment Analyser showing
Investment in Property (left column)
versus   Cash (right column)

Good clients of ours contacted me early in May one year after their accountant had told them they were up for a lot of income tax again. They run a roadhouse in a country town, and had recently built extra motel rooms on to the existing buildings. They had also opened a video department.

When they came to see me I sold them additional real estate worth $300,000. By taking equity out of four of the nine properties they already owned, and applying some of their cash resources, they purchased two luxury 4-bedroom, 2-bathroom townhouses in a triplex complex in Scarborough overlooking a park.

2 and 3/2 Albermarle Street

The properties were settled on 29 June. That same day they paid the next twelve months' interest in advance (receiving a commercial consideration) and therefore had one day's rent to count as income and 366 days' expenses. What did that do to their taxable income? It blew it away. Not only did we kill the tax on their personal income, we also eradicated provisional tax and the 12 per cent surcharge, which applied at that time. Furthermore, they were starting to pick up capital growth on additional real estate worth $300,000.

What happened the following year? Naturally they paid the next year's interest in advance also, though of course the savings weren't as great as in the first year. The tax saved and the rent they received actually paid the interest in the following year and subsequent years.

I put this proposal together myself, but it is just the sort of exercise that an investment analyst might work on. If you offer clients the choice of paying 17 to 47 per cent tax, or 6 to 7.5 per cent interest plus a relatively small amount of tax, they are quite likely to be very interested, especially if they are in one of the higher tax brackets.

If they ever make tax tax deductible, I will consider paying more.

Looking Deeper

I repeat my statement at the head of this chapter: Every real estate firm should have an investment analyst. The investment analyst looks deeper. How many smaller investors would like to buy commercial property? In my experience, more than you might think. How many people have a spare million dollars sitting idle in the bank waiting for you? Surprisingly, perhaps, there are some. How much do they really need to keep there? Very little, and it's up to you to convince them of this.

There are various strategies that investment analysts can use in appropriate circumstances in order to facilitate sales. Here are a couple of examples:

Strata Titling

They could look at strata titling a shopping centre. Suppose one is on the market for $1,000,000: perhaps it could be strata titled into say ten individual shops, each worth $100,000. Do the purchasers need $100,000? No. How much do they need? Nothing, if they have sufficient equity in their own homes.

Landlord's Equity

A vendor can be asked how he is going to use the proceeds from the sale. Perhaps he can be persuaded to leave money in the property as a first, second or third mortgage on vendor's terms. We have done dozens of sales on this basis.

Tax Review

Although we have the experience to be very confident about the proposals we make, I still advise clients to refer them to their own financial planner or accountant. We are only advising them of different options that are available. One thing we do emphasise is that everyone should be looking at their tax in April or May of the current year instead of four to eight months after the gate is closed, i.e. after 30 June.

Creative Developments

Here are some further examples of how the type of creativity an investment analyst can bring to a real estate office led to the generation of substantial business for our firm.

In February 1981 we sold to Chervil Pty Ltd three blocks of double-brick-and-tile flats in Scarborough of twelve, twenty-one and ten units respectively, plus a block of eight 2-bedroom units and one house (all on one title) in Joondanna. We then got the job of arranging strata titling and on-selling all fifty-two units individually. This was excellent business already, but more was to follow. Having initially secured the property management of all units, we went on to retain many of these after the sale, most having been sold to investors.

Perfect examples of
creative developements

Top: 55 Deanmore Rd.
           block of 21 units
Middle: 52 Sackville Tce.
           block of 12 units
Bottom: 47, Deanmore Rd.
           block of 10 units

Creativity came to the fore when we were putting together a development on the corner of Olcote and Ramsdale Streets in Doubleview. Number 31 Ramsdale Street was owned by Les Paxton, our plumbing contractor at the time, and his wife. When we approached them regarding their interest in replacing their existing home with a new one, Mr Paxton mentioned that their neighbour Mrs Kux, of 29 Ramsdale Street, was interested in obtaining a new 3-bedroom unit. We looked into the feasibility of amalgamating the two blocks, but found that we would be very restricted in what we could do. Further inquiries revealed that an adjoining property at 3 Olcote Street was available for purchase, which would give us the scope to create a ten-unit development.

A very creative development at the corner of
Olcote and Ramsdale Streets in Doubleview

According to a legal agreement we entered into with Mr and Mrs Paxton and Mrs Kux, we supplied them with alternative accommodation until the new complex was completed, covered all their costs and incorporated into the development new units designed and built to their requirements. With their titles unencumbered, we were able to borrow enough money to acquire 3 Olcote Street and fund the entire development. This created large savings to the Paxtons and Mrs Kux as well as to us as developers.

When we listed a block of eight flats in Scarborough I put a proposal to my then business partner that we should buy it. He said he would very much like to, but we didn't have the funds available. I then approached the owner and asked him if he had earmarked the proceeds. He said he had not, so I went on to inquire whether he could be interested in keeping one-third while we bought the other two-thirds. He wanted me to explain further.

Initial block of eight,
246 West Coast Hwy, Scarborough

We subsequently made an offer to buy two-thirds of the block. On a net figure, no commission was claimed and all disclosures were done. He left one-third equity in the project, and we borrowed our two-thirds as a first mortgage against the same property. We took on the management. The original owner received his third of the net rent each

Surfside holiday units

month, while we would each receive a third of the rent and add the difference needed to pay the mortgage repayments. The rates and other outgoings were all shared equally. This was still positive gearing for the previous owner, since he owned his one-third outright, whereas our two-thirds was negative gearing, since our expenses were greater than our income (rent).

We gave personal guarantees to the third party also, and a legal document was drawn up clarifying that, if the property was sold, the first mortgagee would get paid first and the original owner next, after which the profits would be split three ways.

Surfside additional 15 units

We then put a syndicate together and bought a further block of fifteen units at the rear of this development, after which we turned all twenty-three into short-term accommodation units. It would not have been a proposition to do this with only the eight units, since one unit in such a set-up has to be used as the manager's quarters, and loss of one-eighth of the income would have meant the project was not viable.

24 Joyce Street

I asked the owners of a block of four flats if they were interested in selling. Each flat had two bedrooms and they were fully furnished. The property was purple titled, meaning that a single title covered the whole group of units. The vendors were not that keen initially: their rental return was not great, but the thought of their money sitting in the bank worried them even more. I suggested they could sell on vendor's terms. The interest rate would be fixed for three years at 13.5 per cent – this ignited a spark of interest – and they would have the same security as a bank over a property they knew well. Now they were keen. I approached a few of my investors, and one cashed-up individual was enthusiastic, but wanted me to consider going in with him. The following took place:

> The owners set their price at $120,000. If we could buy the property for $117,000 and had a mortgage of $90,000 on the terms I had already offered to the vendor, we would need a deposit of $27,000. The investor was keen enough to put up this amount as deposit.

We worked out that I would pay 50 per cent of the interest on $90,000 at 13.5 per cent and 50 per cent of the interest on $27,000 at 10 per cent, the other 50 per cent being his share. I would charge management fees at 10 per cent on his two units. These figures were adjusted and paid monthly. We also had an agreement that, if the property was sold, the first mortgagee (naturally) would be paid the first $90,000, the next $27,000 would go to the investor and the balance – that is, the profits – would be shared equally between the investor and us.

A large property developer owned outright a purple-titled triplex development that we had sold them previously. The client needed funds but was not keen to sell the whole development. For our part we needed to reduce our tax further, so I proposed we buy one-third of the development. They asked how this would work.

I told them that what I envisaged was arranging a mortgage for $40,000 (one-third of $120,000) with the property as security, our position at the time being such that we did not want to put in any money. We would not charge real estate commission, and we would pay the transfer fee on the one-third we were purchasing and

38 Filburn Street

stamp duty on $40,000. Full disclosures were made. Apart from receiving the money they needed, they would continue to derive the positive cash flow from the rentals on two of the units. Their two-thirds of the property was positive gearing, as the only outgoings were shire rates, water rates and land tax. In the deal that we struck, we would manage the development free of charge.

As we had to pay interest on the $40,000 we borrowed as well as our share of the rates and land tax, and one-third of the rental income amounted to substantially less than this total, we would be into negative gearing.

A few years later the same client approached us about our possibly buying the other two-thirds of the property. We reassessed its value and determined that it had increased sufficiently for us to be able to refinance the lot, and we paid them out without any cash input. Once again, no commission was paid and full disclosures were made. The deal created further tax deductibility for us.

Buying Signals

Here is the story of my present office. Originally a picture theatre, in 1981 it was the headquarters of YMCA Scarborough. When Robyn said she was taking our young son Jarrad to gym at the YMCA, I assumed the classes were being held there, but she told me that they took place at the North Beach Hall. Why, when they owned premises

Headquarters of YMCA Scarborough

in Scarborough Beach Road, would they be using a hall some distance to the north? Perhaps they were planning to sell.

I telephoned the YMCA head office and talked to four different people before finally being referred to one of the directors, Mrs Florence Borshopp. It happened that I already knew her, since she was herself a real estate agent. When I asked if they wanted to sell the building in Scarborough, her response was that I must have been psychic, as this very matter was on the agenda for discussion at a meeting that night.

I told her we would buy it, which rather surprised her. It's an old concrete block with an asbestos roof, she said, and you don't even know how much it will be. Anyway she came back with a figure of $120,000 and we bought it. People asked us what we were going to do with an old picture theatre. I told them someone would rent it, to which the reply was: Who would want to rent that place? I said, 'If I knew that, everyone would have bought it.'

How much money did we need? The deposit was $12,000, which left an amount of $108,000 to borrow. The property was leased to the Foursquare Gospel Church and they set it up as 'Potters House'. Positive gearing was created with the rent I negotiated. To put us back into losses, we had to borrow a second mortgage of $20,000.

```
Deposit              12,000
Second mortgage      20,000
Our input was now   ($8,000)
```

This creativity put the property back to a negative situation, and Potters House stayed for approximately seventeen years.

Today it is our real estate office. O'Rourke Realty Investments operates from here and our weekly investment seminars are held on the premises. When we bought the property we never knew we would need our own theatre. The rear of the building is leased to the Billy Weston Pool Hall.

Let's say the value of this property today is $620,000, an increase of $500,000. What does that amount to in terms of return on investment? On the basis of minus $8,000 input, that is 4,000,000 per cent return, divided by twenty years is 200,000 per cent per annum. How does this compare to bank interest? How much is taxed? Does the pool hall help pay the bills? Will the property ever go up in value again?

O'Rourke Realty Investment offices

Is any capital gains tax payable? In this case, no. The property was purchased in 1981, prior to the introduction of capital gains tax in 1985. Of course the same benefit does not apply to current purchases, but it is not all bad news, as I will show.

More Creative Developments

A group of six units was built at 26–28 Ostend Road, Scarborough, by a major national builder for what was a large building society at the time. Another agent had the units listed for a period of three months but did not make a sale. I sold all of them in eighteen hours. How was it done?

Example: **Unit 1, 26-28 Ostend Road, Scarborough**

Purchase price (Investment property)					$79,950
Funding – equity					15,950
– Debt (at 16% fixed for 5 years)					64,000
Gross rental income in year 1 @ $140.00 per week					7,280

Assume 10% growth
Outgoing – 30% of gross income

	Year 1	Year 2	Year 3	Year 4	Year 5	
Income	7,280	8,008	8,808	9,688	10,657	
Outgoing	2,184	2,402	2,642	2,906	3,197	
Interest	10,240	10,240	10,240	10,240	10,240	
	12,424	12,642	12,882	13,146	13,437	
Negative Cash Flow	5,144	4,634	4,074	3,458	2,780	(-$20,090)

Assume 15% per annum capital growth
Assume 11% per annum inflation

	Year 1	Year 2	Year 3	Year 4	Year 5
Capital Value	91,943	105,734	121,594	139,833	160,808
Inflation Value	88,745	98,507	109,343	121,371	134,722

26-28 Ostend Road, Scarborough – **All sold in 18 hours**

Adjusted Real Capital Gain			26,086
	Adjusted capital gain	26,086	
	Less accumulated gearing loss	20,090	
	Therefore capital gains tax on	5,996 (only if sold)	

Overview:

Initial investment equity	15,950	
Establishment costs	3,050	19,000
Capital gain (over 5 years)		80,858
Less negative cash flow		20,090
Actual gain		60,768
Annual average		12,154

Return on investment = $\frac{12{,}154}{19{,}000}$ x 100% = 64.0% **TAX FREE**

Tax formula from 17 July 1985
The tax implications at the point of sale are as follows:
Against the capital gains tax of $5,996
You have the following deductions –

20% of establishment costs each year	3,050
	$2,946
Depreciation on chattels at 20% per annum	3,000
	($ 54)

In addition, tax deduction against other income
4% depreciation on rental accommodation on all new buildings
constructed since 17 July 1985.

Example:	Purchase price	$79,950
	Land content	29,950
	Building content	50,000

4% of $50,000 = $2,000 per annum

This amount is deducted annually for 25 years or for the length of time the investment property is
held as an investment, **AGAINST YOUR OTHER INCOME.**

In summing up, this client was not even in the market to buy real estate, but he needed to reduce his tax. What better way is there to reduce tax and also pick up capital growth? Naturally our office acquired more sales and more property managements as a result of this deal.

305 Harborne Street, Glendalough

The market was down in 1986 and a client of mine needed to sell one of two units in a complex at 305 Harborne Street, Glendalough. I said I would buy it if they would carry me for a second mortgage of $1,400 for two years. I would pay them the $1,400 plus 10 per cent interest for each of the two years in November 1988. With the going commission at $1,000, I would naturally receive that amount or pay $1,000 less.

The contract was drawn up. Purchase price was $24,000 and the deposit was $2,400. A first mortgage of $21,600 was arranged. The second mortgage of $1,400 was registered after settlement. We rented the property out for the two years. By November 1988 the market had exploded following the stock market crash of October 1987, since those who still had resources after the crash were pouring their money back into good old bricks and mortar. The value of the unit by this time was $53,000.

We sold the property for that figure. What was the return? You can't make mathematical sense of such a question on zero input. So what is $30,000 return on $1.00 input? The answer is 30,000 per cent or 15,000 per cent per annum. When the sale took place, the bank got their $21,600 and the original vendor got his $1,400 plus interest at 10 per cent, which amounted to $1,680. This left $29,720.

The beauty of real estate is that **the capital growth is on the total value**, whereas with most investments the return is on your input.

Comfortably Living off Capital Growth

C.N. Darch
211 Abbett Street
SCARBOROUGH WA 6019

20th December 2001

Rental incomes from eight properties, capital wealth in excess of $250 000 and NO TAX!

To Whom it may concern,

Rory O'Rourke was introduced to my wife Tish and myself when we attended one of his free Investment seminars on the 16th August 1995. We had attended numerous investment and get rich quick seminars before, and paid out a lot of money over the years, but Rory's free seminar and his passion and knowledge of his subject, far surpassed any others.

With the knowledge he has gained over 35 years, he is putting into practice what he preaches, and helping us, and many others, to create wealth.

With Rory's help, we have purchased eight properties since meeting him. With Rory's advice we are now comfortably living off our capital growth, and looking forward to an exciting future after just completing our first development. Our capital wealth this year alone is in excess of Two Hundred and Fifty thousand dollars $250,000.00, which far surpassed any previous business income we had.

Even with these properties, and rental incomes we are not taxed – Rory has helped us set up tax structures to minimise the tax we pay.

We have found Rory to be an honest and sincere person, who has helped us through giving us sound and ethical advice.

We would recommend his services to everyone, and our only regret is that it was only six years ago that we met him and not thirty six!!

Thanks Rory,

Yours sincerely,

Darch.

O'Rourke
O'Rourke Realty Investments

A typical investor was looking at cheap units because his bank interest was too low. He was also considering building a spec home in the Morley area. I suggested he should build a triplex in Scarborough. He laughed. Two days later he signed up.

I showed him around the Scarborough area with the emphasis on duplexes and triplexes currently under construction and a few recently finished and sold. All of them were developers' projects.

This particular investor was seventy-three years old. The builder was eighty! I had dealt with the builder for twenty years, and had sold hundreds of units for him. He had a triplex and a duplex under construction and wanted to get another one going to keep his tradesmen working, whereas the investor needed to get his money working for him. The subsequent legal arrangement produced a 'win win win' for both parties and for me.

6

Finance – The Choices

Finance today is a specialty all of its own, which is one reason why your firm needs an investment analyst/coordinator There are many different ways of financing a deal. Some of the sources are:

- banks – client's own bank, his company's bankers, his parents' bankers, our bankers, etc.
- building societies
- merchant banks – normally used only on the bigger deals: commercial, industrial etc.
- mortgage brokers – now doing 50 per cent of Australian residential real estate lendings
- major private lenders – Superannuation Board, University of WA, Anglican Church etc.
- insurance companies/brokers – huge market
- credit unions
- finance companies (long term) – AGC, Esanda, etc.
- bridging finance companies
- vendor's terms – first mortgage, second mortgage, third mortgage
- equity borrowings

Too often we don't analyse what the client intends doing with the proceeds; too often we don't ask what equity he has in his property. As examples in this book show, the client himself can be a very useful source of finance.

Samples of the O'Rourke Bank Qualification follow, a user-friendly program, teamed with the O'Rourke Investment Analyser giving you comprehensive finance tools.

"Bank Qualification" Software

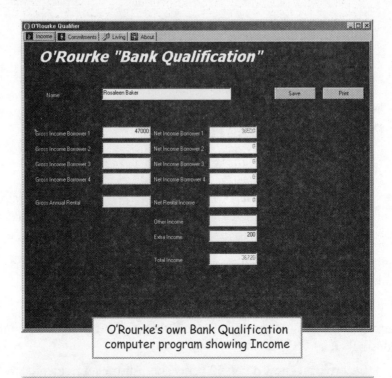

O'Rourke's own Bank Qualification
computer program showing Income

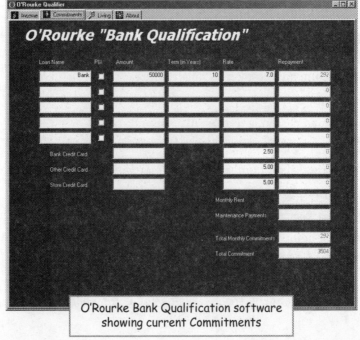

O'Rourke Bank Qualification software
showing current Commitments

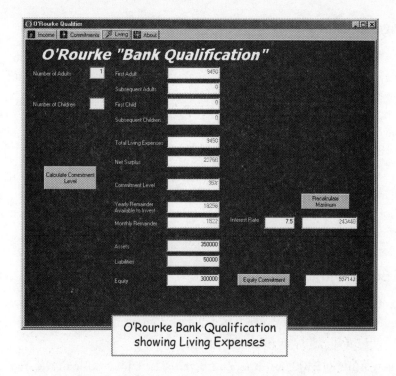

O'Rourke Bank Qualification
showing Living Expenses

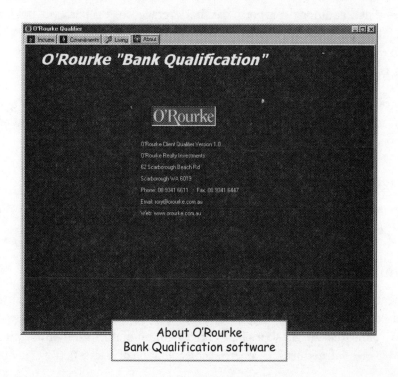

About O'Rourke
Bank Qualification software

Mortgage Brokers

These days, I generally prefer to use a mortgage broker when I organise finance. Mortgage brokers have changed over the years. Originally we had to pay procurement fees when we borrowed through mortgage brokers. Today, the lender pays out of their profits. The broker, who generally represents twenty-five to thirty different lenders, only gets paid if he sets the deal. Because he knows the client is shopping around for the best deal, very often he will find it.

The term 'mortgage broker' has become tainted in recent times, especially in Western Australia, where a major inquiry has uncovered the misuse of millions of dollars of pooled mortgage funds. This should not blind us to the useful role brokers can play in arranging finance for investment property purchases.

Equity Borrowing

What is equity borrowing? Most banks will lend up to 80 per cent of the value of the family home. Even money borrowed on a client's own home is tax deductible as long as it is borrowed for investment purposes.

A home is worth say $300,000 unencumbered. The bank will loan the owner 80 per cent of the value, or $240,000. With leveraging or gearing they can purchase additional properties. Each additional property can be leveraged to 80 per cent borrowings as well, i.e. 80 per cent of the purchase price.

Over-65s

Even our over-65s can now borrow funds against their own homes, and do not need to pay the principal or any interest. The debt will grow until they are deceased and when their property is sold, the lender will be paid out.

Mortgage Insurance

Mortgage insurance is not required if you do not borrow more than 80 per cent of the value of the property.

Prepayment of Interest – Commercial Consideration

Prepayment of interest – i.e. prepaying next year's interest on 29 June of the current year – should be considered if the client is in the upper tax bracket. This allows it to be deducted against the current year's tax. The maximum of thirteen months' prepayment is allowed. Banks will deduct a commercial consideration of at least 0.10 per cent discount

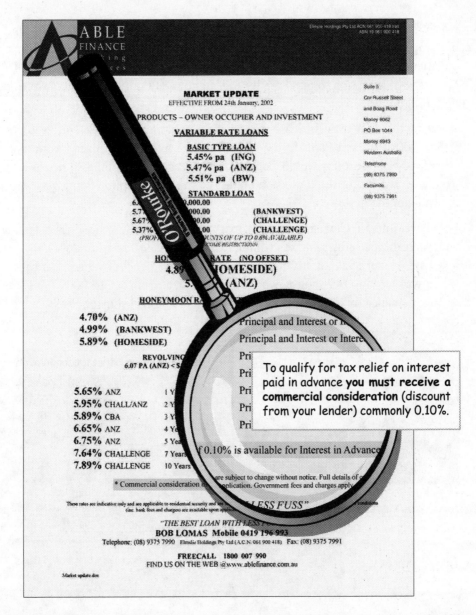

in recognition of the fact that the interest has been paid in advance, but clients should make sure they ask for it. If they don't get the discount, prepayment of interest is deemed to be tax avoidance.

309 Harborne Street, Glendalough

I conclude this chapter with a story about how sometimes rigid financing rules can stand in the way of a perfectly reasonable proposition. But persistence paid off in the end.

No. 309 Harborne Street was a large commercial complex on six acres of land. The buildings were two old aircraft hangars previously used by Duncan Motors. On carrying out a feasibility study on this property in 1972, we found there was a lease to Duncan Motors with an option to purchase for the sum of $84,000. My thoughts were that the option figure was low.

We wanted to take over the lease as long as we could take over the option to purchase at $84,000. I walked Perth trying to pre-arrange finance, but every bank and every other financial institution would loan only 80 per cent of the purchase price or valuation, whichever was the lesser. It did not interest them that the option figure was way below the value of the day.

I tried over thirty lenders until I came across Mr Frank Dart-Kelly, a switched-on financier with Mercantile Credit, who was willing to look at the deal providing we could present him with a sworn valuation through one of his firm's panel of valuers. As I recall, the valuer was Mr John Deephouse, who came up with a figure of $157,000. Mr Dart-Kelly arranged finance for the full purchase price plus the establishment costs.

309 Harborne Street, Glendalough

7

Deposits – Do They Need One?

Where do deposits come from? Aside from cash monies, they can come from any number of sources – equity in home, equity in business, insurance (loan value), shares (loan value), trust units (loan value), boat (sale value), luxury car (down trade), credit union, investment property (part equity) or a family member such as a grandparent, parent, sister, brother, uncle or aunt.

The question can be put another way. How much money does a person need today for a deposit to buy real estate? The answer is nil! Ranging from the first-home buyer with his $7,000 or $10,000 government grant to the second-home buyer who has substantial equity in her own home to the person who has large equity, who needs a deposit. Most of our sales today are created by us showing people how they can buy additional property without having to find any money. The deposit generally comes from equity borrowings against a client's existing home/s.

What Use is Cash…?

What cash monies do your clients really have? It's not necessarily the same as the size of the deposit they would like to pay. Recently I had a couple wanting to pay the minimum deposit on a property purchase – they had 5 per cent firmly lodged in their minds. I emphasised over and over again that it was not a good idea to borrow more than they needed to. It's no good paying 7.75 per cent on a mortgage, I said, and getting 2 per cent on the money you have in the bank. Eventually they saw the point, and were suddenly talking of a $40,000 deposit on a $68,000 property. With this new information I changed tack, and the next day they signed up for two extra properties. So instead of selling them one property I sold them three – and I'll be following up in six to twelve months with a good chance of selling them more.

...or Equity?

Most of my sales are for investment purposes. If someone says they own their own home, I ask them what it is worth. They might say $300,000. I ask them how old their mattress is, and possibly they'll say five years. I follow up with another question: Is it firm or bumpy? They wonder what I'm getting at until I tell them they have $300,000 stuffed in it. Where did they learn this? From their grandparents. People of that generation didn't trust banks, so they hid their money under the mattress. We are doing the same. (What FID or BAD taxes did they pay on the money under the mattress? Were they smarter than us?)

Granny may have hidden her money under the mattress – but have you got yours stuffed in your mattress?

Equity in Home

If the value of the average house doubles every seven years, it is not hard to see that a great number of people have untouched equity in their homes. We have the opportunity to show them how to utilise it to buy additional property while reducing their tax and increasing their wealth.

Equity in Business

Your client has been in business for fifteen to twenty years. He is a panel beater in his own premises in an industrial zone. Is he really working to his capacity? The value of his property is probably growing faster each year than his net profit in the business. If he has been there for that length of time, he possibly owns the premises freehold. If so, he could utilise some of this equity to buy additional properties. Thus he could reduce the business profits and thereby reduce the tax payable by the business, these purchases will create additional capital wealth.

You need to further qualify whether it is a company, partnership, trust or whatever, and whether a separate entity should be set up as the owner of the property, rather than the operating company, so that you can further move the figures around. (Are you comfortable in these areas? Perhaps you need an investment coordinator in your office.)

Other Sources

Most life policies can be borrowed against – in some cases up to as much as 90 per cent of the total premiums paid. You need to have a look at all your client's other policies also.

Just as you can negative gear real estate, you can negative gear stocks and shares. Why not suggest to your client that they borrow against their share portfolio to buy real estate? They can have the best of both worlds: most people are reluctant to sell their shares, and this way they do not have to.

As with shares, trust units can be negatively geared to buy real estate. If the trust units have gone up in value say three or four times, suggest to your client taking out the original purchase price by borrowing to create additional capital for real estate investment. All monies borrowed for investment purposes are tax deductible.

How many times do you come across a purchaser who says they would love to buy if only they had the money? Here's a suggestion that could be appropriate for some: suggest to them that they sell the boat and buy real estate. The real estate goes up in value, and then they can buy another boat. Or, if he owns a luxury car, you could suggest that he sells it, buys a bomb and gets into real estate. By doing this he would have freed up capital for the all-important deposit and reduced his repayments at the same time, increasing his capacity to repay. Suddenly we have a qualified buyer. What will we sell him?

Paying Off Principal

Then there is the case of the client, or potential client, who is paying principal and interest over a short term. They are paying off a lot of principal, and this is not tax deductible. What is their current equity? Might it be possible to take some equity out of their existing home to buy an investment property, and rearrange matters so that the greater part of their monthly payments are tax deductible? Quite possibly they will not have to pay any more to have two properties, rather than just one, appreciating in value.

No-Deposit Deals for First-Home Owners

If your client says they have no assets, do they know all the government grants that are available? At least until the middle of 2002 the following grants are available – $7,000 on established homes, $10,000 for new homes and up to $2,000 government assistance towards their legal costs. These are for first-home purchasers and new approved migrants.

The Bank's Attitude

A bank will sometimes take the attitude that, if the family won't help, why should we take the risk? If people have no track record in borrowing, why should the bank take the chance? So how could a family member help?

- by gifting them a deposit
- by buying jointly with them
- by buying the property and leasing it to them while reducing their own tax

Does the relative need money? Not necessarily: they can borrow against the equity in their own home.

Finding that deposit can sometimes be a challenge, but often it's just a matter of looking a bit deeper, being a little more creative, **thinking outside the square**.

Buying Property with No Deposit

Is it possible to buy property with no deposit? Here's documentation of a case where I did just that. All I paid up front to buy three Scarborough properties was $250.50 stamp duty.

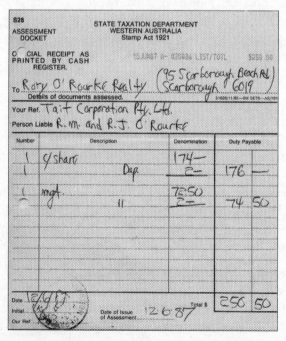

R.J.O'Rourke
9 Belhus Drive
Trigg
December 16th 1986

Tait Corporation
381 West Coast Hwy
Trigg

Dear Michael,

Following our meeting at 3.30pm on December 15th 1986, I wish to submit
the following offer for the purchase of Tait Corporation:

I am prepared to offer twenty nine thousand dollars ($29,000.00) and
understand that the assets which will remain in the company are the
three properties:

    Unit 4   27 Filburn Ave   Scarborough
    Unit 5   186 West Coast Hwy   Scarborough
    Unit 7   276 West Coast Hwy   Scarborough

I understand the full details of the mortgages carried by these three
units. I wish you to loan me for two (2) years twenty nine thousand
dollars commencing from February 28th 1987, this being the date we
have agreed upon when mortgage payments will be taken over by me. I
further undertake to make quarterly interest payments at fifteen percent
(15%) represented by one thousand and eighty seven dollars and fifty
cents ($1,087.50) per quarter as follows:

28th May 1987   28th August 1987   28th Nov 1987   28th Feb 1988
28th May 1988   28th Auhgust 1988   28th Nov 1988   28th Feb 1989

The last interest payment will be accompanied by the repayment of the
principal ($29,000.00).

Legal and stamp duty costs will be paid by me and you will provide
a set of accounts and financial statement for Tait Corporation up to
December 31st 1986.

I would appreciate your signing the enclosed copy of this offer to
signify your acceptance from December 15th 1986.

Yours sincerely,

                                    I accept this offer Michael V Tait

                                    Date   16-2-87

                                    Witness

Rory O'Rourke   Richard Whitton
                                           58 Sorrento St
                                           North Beach
                                           6020

> We took over the company Tait Corporation which owned the three properties. The cost was $250.50 stamp duty.

Above – Unit 4/27 Filburn Street
Scarborough

Above – Unit 7/276
West Coast Highway
Scarborough

Right – Unit 5/186
West Coast Highway
Scarborough

8

Debt Versus Death

Debt and death – these two words sound very similar. Debt and death scare all of us. But should they? Death could be bad, depending on your individual beliefs, but there can be little question about debt. Can you name a wealthy person or corporation that doesn't have debt? Obviously they aren't scared of it. Neither you nor your clients need to be either. Debt is good; debt is best.

What assets would you have today if someone hadn't loaned you money in the first place? Debt is normally short to medium term. Let's consider the relevance by looking at the case of my own family home:

1979 property value	$ 48,000
1979 property mortgage	$ 38,000
1979 deposit	$ 10,000
1979 equity	$ 10,000
2002 property value	$1,500,000
2002 mortgage still	$ 38,000
2002 equity	$1,462,000

> ### Value Qualification
> 1 December 2001, Mick Malone Real Estate auctioned
> 10 Muller Street, North Beach. This 506 m² block realised $825,000.
> 9 Belhus Drive, Trigg (my family home) is a 974 m² block.

Making Use of Equity

All of us should have an equity facility to cover us for a rainy day. But here is a case of equity amounting to nearly $1.5 million. Could we do more? What we have done over the years is create progressively greater equity borrowings in line with the increasing value of the home. With them we have been able to buy more income-producing properties and prepay the interest twelve months in advance on each of them, thus reducing that year's tax. Did we care that we had more debt? No.

A million thanks to Mary

big weekend Saturday March 17, 2001

"Always be in debt. It is the only way to make money."

Mary Raine (née Carter)

In a bid to improve her childhood circumstances, Mary Carter moved to Australia in the 1900s. When she died in Perth in 1960, she left a million-pound estate which was used to set up the Raine Medical Research Foundation. Pam Casellas traces her story.

When Mary died in Perth in 1960 she left an estate valued at one million pounds, a huge sum for the time. And so began the Raine Medical Research Foundation, which celebrates its 40th anniversary on Thursday. The foundation has plenty to celebrate beyond reaching that milestone. It is the State's biggest non-government provider of medical research funds and should also feel free to celebrate the fact that the estate has grown $24 million and has contributed a total of 18 million for research.

Mary Carter, who later became Ma Thomas and finally Mary Raine made her fortune from buying and selling Perth real estate in the early part of the century and consolidating that with canny acquisition and management of some of the city's early hotel and commercial landmarks. Best known of these were the Wentworth Hotel, the United Services Hotel and the South Perth landmark, the Windsor Hotel.

Mary recognised in the 1900s that to make money you had to be in debt. Today, her philosophy makes even more sense. It is almost impossible to create substantial wealth without getting into debt. (Reproduced by courtesy of *The West Australian*)

When is Debt Good?

What are banks doing all day every day? They are borrowing money. We have been brought up to believe they lend money. Yes, there is some truth in that, but first they had to borrow it. When was the last time you remember a bank saying they had enough money, and wouldn't be borrowing any more because it was too risky?

What's the main security the banks want? Real Estate every time.

Debt is good as long as it is income-producing real estate.

9

Time Management is Money Management

Have you ever wondered about your parents sending you to school for ten or twelve years so you could learn how to work for the rest of your life so you could have a three-year holiday before you die?

That's one reflection about the future; now here's another. I hate to be the bearer of bad news, but you are not going to get a pension like your parents did. You will have to continue working until you die or pay for your own retirement.

Why have the majority of us stopped experimenting as we grow older? As children we experimented with everything, from crying when we wanted attention to eating snails. As adults most of us have got ourselves into a rut and forgotten to ask ourselves **WHY**.

Our Use of Time

Time management is money management. We each have twenty-four hours a day available to us. We work eight to ten hours, which leaves fourteen to sixteen hours. What do we do with them? We eat, we sleep, we watch television, perhaps read. Is it any wonder we are poor? That's our own time we have wasted, and it can never be replaced.

We have spent say nine hours per day working for someone else, increasing their efficiency and profitability. When it comes to managing the change we are left with after the tax man takes his slice, we do nothing about it. Isn't this an indictment against ourselves? Could we not put one or two hours a day into managing our assets? Instead, we normally hand our surplus over to a bank teller. (Have you ever wondered where he or she is in the banking system?) Or we give it to an insurance salesman or an investment adviser. What do they do with it? Are they smarter/wealthier than us?... No. Why did we give them our hard-earned money?

Motivation

Motivation must come from within. As humans we dream a lot, but we don't often take the action that could make those dreams come true. If we are not willing to help ourselves, who will do it for us? I have helped hundreds of people achieve their dreams or goals through my weekly wealth-creation seminars. But it is up to them to act.

A few years ago I had just sold an industrial property 25 Wellard Street, Bibra Lake to a major client for $900,000. I was about to take my departure from the CEO when he asked me about the seminars he knew I had been running. He told me I had fifteen minutes to present him with a summary. Seeing I had just made in excess of $20,000 commission, I thought I could certainly give him fifteen minutes, so I started a mini seminar for him. He ended up cancelling three other appointments, and an hour and a half later we were still talking. He said, 'Rory, you are talking about me. I spend my entire day worrying about my 350 staff, my shareholders and my directors in three different companies. When it comes to managing my own assets, there is no time left. I need you to assist me in managing them.'

He put me in touch with his company secretary. Naturally this man was smarter and richer than his boss? No. He did not have the time to talk to a real estate agent. (Is that really the role I am playing today? I don't think so.) So he put me on to their new company accountant, who was about twenty-four years of age and had been top of his class – but that didn't make him street-wise. Two years later we still haven't done any additional business.

Good ideas don't always get through the ranks. Here was an instance of directions from the CEO not getting activated for the benefit of all. Apart from my taking a role in the management of his personal assets, he had been looking to setting up an in-house superannuation scheme built around real estate for the benefit of the staff, the directors and himself, with our firm acquiring the property portfolio and then managing the properties. Perhaps, if he'd given it just a little more time while his mind was focused on it, that firm might now have a thriving super scheme.

Do we need to be slaves to our own homes? Here is a case of a couple who were sitting on a goldmine, but hadn't put the time and thought into managing their assets creatively:

Some twenty years ago I was asked to appraise a City Beach home. The property was worth approximately $650,000. I asked the owner, who was the managing director of a large company in Osborne Park, whether he liked baby-sitting, bottle-washing, cleaning, cooking, housekeeping and washing the car. His reply was, 'We are a long way past baby-sitting and bottle-washing, and I don't do any of the others'. His wife, who was in the kitchen, called out to say she did them. I asked if she liked that kind of work, and her reply was, 'No, but someone has to do it'. I told her there was no need for her to do those jobs. That got her attention.

They owned that property and a farm outright. I suggested that, if they sold City Beach for $650,000, the money could be invested into $2 million worth of income-producing real estate. If this increased in value by 10 per cent per year, that would amount to a gain of $200,000 annually. With that money available, I could put them up in an international hotel at a special rate of say $1,000 a week, or $52,000 for the year. I could have thrown in a cleaner, all meals and a chauffeur-driven limousine and not used up a huge part of the balance. I asked the lady of the house whether, if her husband gave her a housekeeping allowance of $148,000 per year, they could live any better. She got the point. We listed and sold their home within a month of that discussion.

Do we necessarily need to own our own homes or have the amount of equity in them most of us have today? The answer is no.

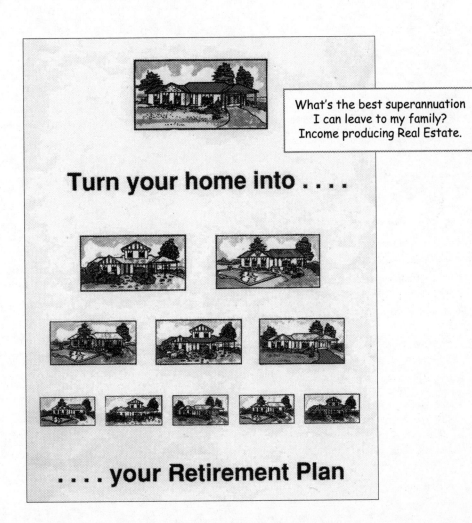

10

Listings are the Name of the Game

If we don't get listings, we have no stock to sell. If we don't sell our marketing ability to the vendor, we don't get the listing. In listing, marketing is the be-all and end-all.

Out of a total commission the listing representative in Western Australia generally earns 60 per cent of the 50 per cent commission split. On residential properties the selling representative gets 40 per cent of the 50 per cent commission split. Out of the total commission, 50 per cent goes to the real estate firm.

The secret is to get the listing. Once I have that, I generally succeed 95 per cent of the time in making the sale. Choose the best marketing approach; work out which method will suit the situation. Don't restrict your options. Private treaty, auctions and tenders – all three have merit.

'List and Last' is as true today as it was a hundred years ago. The phone doesn't ring unless you have listings. If your phone doesn't ring, it can only be a matter of time before you are out of business.

Sell Opposition's Stock

You should always sell at least three of the opposition's stock prior to selling your actual listing. That way you will get to know the comparable properties available and understand their pluses and minuses.

Acquiring Knowledge

With every enquiry you receive, ask questions. The more questions we ask the more we find out. The more knowledge we have, the more we can help. If we help the client, we help ourselves.

Why do clients buy properties? I have sold literally hundreds of properties on behalf of the Martinovich and Rainoldi families. Why did the Rainoldi family buy a shopping centre and some office units in June 1982? For tax reasons.

By buying the Station Street Shopping Centre in Cottesloe and five office units at Kobold House in West Perth, and prepaying the interest twelve months in advance, the Rainoldis reduced their taxable income substantially – and so also reduced their provisional tax and the 12 per cent surcharge that applied at the time.

BALANCING A MAJOR INVESTMENT PORTFOLIO

Perth real estate investors G.J. and J.G. Rainoldi have updated their investment portfolio with the purchase through Mal Dempsey & Associates of the Station Street Shopping Centre in Cottesloe.

Mr Jack Rainoldi said he had wanted to ensure that the portfolio had an even spread of commercial, residential and office properties.

In a note of appreciation to the company, Mr Rainoldi said: "We would like to take the opportunity to thank you for your assistance with our numerous real estate transactions over the past three years. There is no doubt the service has been second to none."

"We have on many occasions inspected our different properties which you manage in our investment portfolio and have always found them to be in good condition."

Mr Jack Rainoldi (left) is pictured with Mal Dempsey and Associates principal Rory O'Rourke handing over the shopping centre.

"We would especially like to thank you for your excellent assistance in the acquisition of the Station Street Shopping Centre and the smooth manner in which you took over its property management. We would like to pass on our appreciation to Mal Dempsey and all members of the staff."

Some twelve months later Mr Rainoldi told me he was not happy with the shopping centre we had sold him. He just wasn't comfortable with shopping centres: he knew residential property better.

Eighteen Sales in a Day

It happened that over the previous three years I had sold an eastern states client seventeen Perth residential properties on behalf of Mr Rainoldi. I telephoned the client and asked if they would be interested in the Station Street Shopping Centre.

They expressed great interest, but went on to say that they had no money available. I suggested an exchange of equities: the seventeen residential properties for the shopping centre. Mr Rainoldi agreed: he bought the seventeen properties back and our eastern states client bought the shopping centre – with certain conditions on each contract.

This meant **eighteen sales in a single day once again**, full commission being received on each. Over the next three months we on-sold the seventeen residential properties once again on behalf of Mr Rainoldi. More commission.

Listings are indeed the name of the game, but this case shows how they can sometimes come relatively easily if you have built up a base of investor clients and are prepared to think creatively.

TO:

Mal Dempsey & Associates Pty Ltd Trading as

MAL DEMPSEY
& ASSOCIATES

Professionals

REAL ESTATE AGENTS — Licensee: M. Dempsey J.P.
95 SCARBOROUGH BEACH RD., SCARBOROUGH
TELEPHONE 341 6611

As Agent for the Vendor(s)

Full name address and occupation

I/WE ..... NANDI HOLDINGS (COOTAMUNDRA) PTY. LTD. AND

..... KANDEHA (HOLDINGS) PTY. LTD.

.... 92 COOPER STREET, COOTAMUNDRA .... ("the Purchaser")

HEREBY OFFER TO PURCHASE (as joint tenants/tenants in common) the land described in the Schedule hereto and all improvements thereon ("the Property") with vacant possession unless otherwise provided in the Conditions together with the Chattels (if any) described in the Schedule at the price and on the other terms set out in the Schedule and subject to the Conditions

SCHEDULE

(i) **Description of property:** The land situated at and known as ....

..... "STATION STREET SHOPPING CENTRE"

..... STATION STREET, COTTESLOE

being Portion of ..... SWAN ..... Location ..... 349 ..... and being Lot 35

XXXXXXXXXXXXXXXX/Diagram ..... 45750 ..... and being the whole/part of the land in

Certificate of Title Volume ..... 1364 ..... Folio 632

(ii) **Purchase Price:** $ 620,000 ..... of which $ ..... - ..... is allocated to chattels.

(iii) **Manner of Payment:** A deposit of $ 30,000 ..... of which $ ..... -
..... "REFER CLAUSE 9"
is paid herewith and $ ..... shall be paid within ..... days of acceptance.

The balance of the purchase price shall be paid on settlement.

(iv) **Settlement Date:** ..... ON OR BEFORE 30-4-1985

(v) **Chattels, including Plant & Equipment:** ..... NIL

....

....

CONDITIONS

Delete if not required by the Purchaser

1. (1.1) This Contract is conditional upon the undermentioned Lender(s), or any other lender(s) acceptable to the Purchaser, approving on or before the latest date for approval specified hereunder, the granting to the Purchaser of a loan(s) of an amount not less than the amount(s) specified.
   (1.2) The Purchaser shall:—
   (a) use his best endeavours to obtain such loan(s)
   and
   (b) notify the Vendor or his Agent in writing of the approval (or otherwise) not later than forty-eight (48) hours after the latest date for approval.
   (1.3) If the condition in paragraph (1.1) hereof shall not be fully satisfied by the latest date for approval then subject to the Purchaser having complied with paragraph (1.2) hereof UNLESS the Purchaser shall have waived this condition and communicated such waiver in writing to the Vendor or his Agent prior to the latest date for approval, then this Contract shall be deemed to have come to an end without the necessity for either party giving notice to that effect, whereupon the deposit and all other moneys (if any) paid hereunder shall forthwith be refunded to the Purchaser and there shall be no further claim under the Contract by either the Vendor or the Purchaser against the other either at law or in equity.
   (1.4) This clause shall operate for the benefit of both the Vendor and the Purchaser.

	First Mortgage	Second Mortgage
Lender:	VENDOR TO CARRY $590,000	
Latest Date for Approval:	N/A	
Amount of Loan:	$590,000	

> This offer and acceptance is me selling Station Street Shopping Centre for the second time. See conditions on the next page.

2. Acceptance of this offer shall be sufficiently communicated to the Purchaser if notification thereof shall be given by the Vendor's Agent to the Purchaser.

3. THE REAL ESTATE INSTITUTE OF WESTERN AUSTRALIA (Inc.) GENERAL CONDITIONS FOR THE SALE OF LAND (1982 REVISION) shall be incorporated herein and shall apply to this sale so far as they are not varied by or inconsistent with the express terms hereof.

(conditions as required to be added hereunder)

4. THIS OFFER IS SUBJECT TO THE VENDOR PURCHASING 17 PROPERTIES AS PER THE ATTACHED OFFER AND ACCEPTANCE.

5. THE VENDOR AGREES TO CARRY THE SUM OF $590,000 AT A RATE OF 16% (INTEREST ONLY) FOR A PERIOD OF TWO YEARS.

6. THE VENDOR AGREES ON THE BASIS OF THE PURCHASER TAKING POSSESSION ON 30TH APRIL 1983, ALL RENTS WILL BE DUE TO THE PURCHASER AS DOES THE LIABILITY OF ALL RATES, MAINTENANCE, MANAGEMENT FEES ETC.

7. THE VENDOR AGREES TO PAY COMMISSION AT R.E.I.W.A. RATES ON THE DATE OF POSSESSION.

8. THE VENDOR AGREES TO CONTINUE THE PAYMENTS ON THE EXISTING MORTGAGES OR REPLACEMENT MORTGAGES FOR THE PERIOD OF THIS CONTRACT.

9. THE DEPOSIT OF $30,000 IS MADE UP OF THE EQUITY IN THE 17 DIFFERENT PROPERTIES.

10. THE VENDOR AGREES TO EXECUTE ANY CONTRACTS OR TRANSFERS NECESSARY, SHOULD THE PURCHASER SELL ALL OR ANY PART TO A THIRD PARTY.

11. THE VENDOR AGREES TO THE REGISTRATION OF THE STRATA TITLE.

Purchaser: _KANSERA (HOLDINGS) P/L DIRECTOR_ Purchaser: _LAND HOLDINGS (AUST) P/L DIRECTOR_

Witness: _____ Witness: _____

Date: 19 / 4 / 83 Date: /83

I/WE GUIDO JOHN RAINOLDI (BUILDER) AND JOHN GERALD RAINOLDI (BUILDER)

of 112 MILLCREST STREET, DOUBLEVIEW WA 6018

("the Vendor") HEREBY ACCEPTS the above offer and acknowledges that the selling fee payable to the Vendor's Agent is my/our responsibility.

Vendor: _____ Vendor: _____

Witness: _____ Witness: _____

Date: 19. 4. 83 Date: 19. 4. 83

The parties respectively appoint the Solicitor or Settlement Agent named hereunder to act on their behalf in respect of this transaction and agree to pay their costs in respect thereto.

Name of Purchaser's Representative   Name of Vendor's Representative

Signature (Purchaser)   Signature (Vendor)

A true copy of this document has been received by each of the signatories hereto—together with a copy of THE REAL ESTATE INSTITUTE OF WESTERN AUSTRALIA (Inc.) GENERAL CONDITIONS FOR THE SALE OF LAND (1982 REVISION).

DATE 20 4 83   DATE 20 4 83

DATE / /   DATE / /

> This shows the purchase is subject to the vendor buying
> 17 properties from the purchaser. These happened to be the same
> 17 I had previously sold to the purchasers on behalf of the vendor.

TO:

Mal Dempsey & Associates Pty Ltd Trading as

MAL DEMPSEY
& ASSOCIATES

Professionals

REAL ESTATE AGENTS—Licensee M Dempsey J.P.
95 SCARBOROUGH BEACH RD., SCARBOROUGH
TELEPHONE 341 6611

As Agent for the Vendor(s)

Full name, address and occupation
I/WE .GUIDO JOHN RAINOLDI. (BUILDER) AND JOHN GERALD RAINOLDI. (BUILDER) ...

..... BOTH OF 112 MILLCREST STREET, DOUBLEVIEW WA 6018 .....

.... ("the Purchaser

HEREBY OFFER TO PURCHASE (as joint tenants/tenants in common) the land described in t
Schedule hereto and all improvements thereon ("the Property") with vacant possession unless oth
wise provided in the Conditions together with the Chattels (if any) described in the Schedule at t
price and on the other terms set out in the Schedule and subject to the Conditions.

SCHEDULE

(i) **Description of property:** The land situated at and known as .UNIT .6.,12,13/189 ......

..... NORTH BEACH DRIVE, TUART HILL .....

....

being Portion of .PERTH .SHIRE Location ..A.:.............and being Lot 6 ,. 12 ,. 13.

on Strata Plan/Plan/Diagram ...2751...............and being the whole/part of the land

Certificate of Title Volume...1391.....Folio 933, .939, .940..

(ii) **Purchase Price:** $ 93,000 .....of which $ 3,000............is allocated to chattels.

(iii) **Manner of Payment:** A deposit of $6,000....................of which $.. .....
        "REFER CLAUSE 6"
is paid herewith and $...........shall be paid within....-.....days of acceptan

The balance of the purchase price shall be paid on settlement.

(iv) **Settlement Date:**...ON. OR. BEFORE. 30-4-1985 ....

(v) **Chattels, including Plant & Equipment:** FLOOR COVERINGS, WINDOW TREATMENTS

....

....

....

CONDITIONS

Delete if not required by the Purchaser

1. (1.1) This Contract is conditional upon the undermentioned Lender(s), or any other lender
   acceptable to the Purchaser, approving on or before the latest date for approval specif
   hereunder, the granting to the Purchaser of a loan(s) of an amount not less than
   amount(s) specified.
   (1.2) The Purchaser shall:—
       (a) use his best endeavours to obtain such loan(s)
           and
       (b) notify the Vendor or his Agent in writing of the approval (or otherwise) not later t
           forty-eight (48) hours after the latest date for approval.
   (1.3) If the condition in paragraph (1.1) hereof shall not be fully satisfied by the latest date
       approval then subject to the Purchaser having complied with paragraph (1.2) hereof UNL
       the Purchaser shall have waived this condition and communicated such waiver in writin
       the Vendor or his Agent prior to the latest date for approval, then this Contract shal
       deemed to have come to an end without the necessity for either party giving notice to
       effect, whereupon the deposit and all other moneys (if any) paid hereunder shall forthwit
       refunded to the Purchaser and there shall be no further claim under the Contract by either
       Vendor or the Purchaser against the other either at law or in equity.
   (1.4) This clause shall operate for the benefit of both the Vendor and the Purchaser.

	First Mortgage	Second Mortgage
Lender:	........................)	....
Latest Date for Approval:	........................) "REFER CLAUSE 7"	....
Amount of Loan:	........................)	....

> This offer is for three of the 17 being re-purchased.

2. Acceptance of this offer shall be sufficiently communicated to the Purchaser if notification thereof shall be given by the Vendor's Agent to the Purchaser.

3. THE REAL ESTATE INSTITUTE OF WESTERN AUSTRALIA (Inc.) GENERAL CONDITIONS FOR THE SALE OF LAND (1982 REVISION) shall be incorporated herein and shall apply to this sale so far as they are not varied by or inconsistent with the express terms hereof.

(conditions as required to be added hereunder)

4. THIS OFFER IS SUBJECT TO THE VENDOR PURCHASING THE STATION STREET SHOPPING CENTRE.

5. THE VENDOR AGREES, ON THE PURCHASER TAKING POSSESSION ON THE 30TH APRIL 1983, ALL RENTS WILL GO TO THE PURCHASER, AS DOES THE LIABILITIES OF ALL RATES, MAINTENANCE, MANAGEMENT FEES ETC.

6. THE DEPOSIT IS MADE UP OF PART EQUITY FROM THE STATION STREET SHOPPING CENTRE (IE. $6,000).

7. THE PURCHASER AGREES TO PAY 16% (P.A.) INTEREST ONLY ON THE AMOUNT OF $87,000 UNTIL SETTLEMENT.

8. THE VENDORS AGREE TO EXECUTE ANY CONTRACTS OR TRANSFERS NECESSARY, SHOULD THE PURCHASER RE-SELL ANY OR ALL OF THE MENTIONED PROPERTIES.

9. THE VENDOR AGREES TO CONTINUE THE PAYMENTS ON THE EXISTING MORTGAGES FOR THE PERIOD OF THIS CONTRACT.

Purchaser: _____   Purchaser: _____

Witness: _____   Witness: _____

Date: 19/4/83   Date: 19/4/83

I/WE   NANDI HOLDINGS (COOTAMUNDRA) PTY. LTD. AND

KANDEHA (HOLDINGS) PTY. LTD.

of   92 COOPER STREET, COOTAMUNDRA

("the Vendor") HEREBY ACCEPTS the above offer and acknowledges that the selling fee payable to the Vendor's Agent is my/our responsibility.

Vendor: _____   Vendor: _____

Witness: _____   Witness: _____

Date: 21/4/83   Date: 21/4/83

The parties respectively appoint the Solicitor or Settlement Agent named hereunder to act on their behalf in respect of this transaction and agree to pay their costs in respect thereto.

Name of Purchaser's Representative   Name of Vendor's Representative

_____   _____

Signature (Purchaser)   Signature (Vendor)

A true copy of this document has been received by each of the signatories hereto—together with a copy of THE REAL ESTATE INSTITUTE OF WESTERN AUSTRALIA (Inc.) GENERAL CONDITIONS FOR THE SALE OF LAND (1982 REVISION).

_____ DATE 19/83   _____ DATE 19/4

_____ DATE 21/4   _____ DATE 21/4

Each of the offers is subject to simultaneous settlement.

TO:

MAL DEMPSEY
& ASSOCIATES

Professionals

Mal Dempsey & Associates Pty. Ltd. Trading as:

REAL ESTATE AGENTS—Licensee: M. Dempsey J.P.
95 SCARBOROUGH BEACH RD., SCARBOROUGH
TELEPHONE 341 6611

As Agent for the Vendor(s)

Full name, address and occupation   I/WE .... GUIDO JOHN RAINOLDI (BUILDER) AND JOHN GERALD RAINOLDI (BUILDER)

.... 112 MILLCREST STREET, DOUBLEVIEW WA 6018 ....

.... ("the Purchaser")

HEREBY OFFER TO PURCHASE (as joint tenants/tenants in common) the land described in the Schedule hereto and all improvements thereon ("the Property") with vacant possession unless otherwise provided in the Conditions together with the Chattels (if any) described in the Schedule at the price and on the other terms set out in the Schedule and subject to the Conditions.

SCHEDULE

(i) **Description of property:** The land situated at and known as.................................

.24 GREEN STREET, JOONDANNA ....

....

being Portion of .. SWAN........ Location .. 3980.............and being Lot ....

on Strata Plan/Plan/Diagram ....and being the whole/part of the land in

Certificate of Title Volume.. 1135..... Folio .. 109 ....

(ii) **Purchase Price:** $ 39,000...... of which $............—..........is allocated to chattels

(iii) **Manner of Payment:** A deposit of $ 3,000 .... of which $ ...—......
     "REFER CLAUSE 6"
     is paid herewith and $ ....shall be paid within................... days of acceptance.

The balance of the purchase price shall be paid on settlement.

(iv) **Settlement Date:**.....ON OR BEFORE 30-4-1985..............

(v) **Chattels, including Plant & Equipment:** . NIL ....

....

....

....

CONDITIONS

1. (1.1) This Contract is conditional upon the undermentioned Lender(s), or any other lender(s) acceptable to the Purchaser, approving on or before the latest date for approval specified hereunder, the granting to the Purchaser of a loan(s) of an amount not less than the amount(s) specified.

(1.2) The Purchaser shall—
   (a) use his best endeavours to obtain such loan(s) and
   (b) notify the Vendor or his Agent in writing of the approval (or otherwise) not later than forty-eight (48) hours after the latest date for approval.

(1.3) If the condition in paragraph (1.1) hereof shall not be fully satisfied by the latest date for approval then subject to the Purchaser having complied with paragraph (1.2) hereof UNLESS the Purchaser shall have waived this condition and communicated such waiver in writing to the Vendor or his Agent prior to the latest date for approval, then this Contract shall be deemed to have come to an end without the necessity for either party giving notice to that effect, whereupon the deposit and all other moneys (if any) paid hereunder shall forthwith be refunded to the Purchaser and there shall be no further claim under the Contract by either Vendor or the Purchaser against the other either at law or in equity.

(1.4) This clause shall operate for the benefit of both the Vendor and the Purchaser.

	First Mortgage	Second Mortgage
Lender:	.............)	....
Latest Date for Approval:	............}	"REFER CLAUSE 7"
Amount of Loan:	.............)	....

Delete if not required by the Purchaser

One house I had previously sold being traded back.

2. Acceptance of this offer shall be sufficiently communicated to the Purchaser if notification thereof shall be given by the Vendor's Agent to the Purchaser.

3. THE REAL ESTATE INSTITUTE OF WESTERN AUSTRALIA (Inc.) GENERAL CONDITIONS FOR THE SALE OF LAND (1982 REVISION) shall be incorporated herein and shall apply to this sale so far as they are not varied by or inconsistent with the express terms hereof.

(conditions as required to be added hereunder)

4. THIS OFFER IS SUBJECT TO THE VENDOR PURCHASING "THE STATION STREET SHOPPING CENTRE".

5. THE VENDOR AGREES ON THE PURCHASER TAKING POSSESSION ON THE 30TH APRIL 1983 ALL RENTS WILL GO TO THE PURCHASER, AS DOES ALL RATES, MAINTENANCE, MANAGEMENT FEES ETC.

6. THE DEPOSIT IS MADE UP FROM PART EQUITY ON THE STATION STREET SHOPPING CENTRE (IE. $3,000).

7. THE PURCHASER TAKES OVER THEIR OWN MRTGAGES UPON POSSESSION.

8. THE VENDOR AGREES TO EXECUTE ANY CONTRACT OR TRANSFER, SHOULD THE PURCHASER WISH TO RE-SELL.

Purchaser: _____   Purchaser: _____

Witness: _____   Witness: _____

Date: _____   Date: _____

I/WE   NANDI HOLDINGS (COOTAMUNDRA) PTY. LTD. AND KANDEHA (HOLDINGS) PTY. LTD.

of   92 COOPER STREET, COOTAMUNDRA

("the Vendor") HEREBY ACCEPTS the above offer and acknowledges that the selling fee payable to the Vendor's Agent is my/our responsibility.

Vendor: _____   DIRECTOR   Vendor: _____   DIRECTOR

Witness: _____   Witness: _____

Date: 21/4/83   Date: 21/4/83

The parties respectively appoint the Solicitor or Settlement Agent named hereunder to act on their behalf in respect of this transaction and agree to pay their costs in respect thereto.

Name of Purchaser's Representative   Name of Vendor's Representative

....

_____ Signature (Purchaser)   _____ Signature (Vendor)

A true copy of this document has been received by each of the signatories hereto—together with a copy of THE REAL ESTATE INSTITUTE OF WESTERN AUSTRALIA (Inc.) GENERAL CONDITIONS FOR THE SALE OF LAND (1982 REVISION)

_____ DATE 19483   _____ DATE 19/4/83

_____ DATE 21483   _____ DATE 21/4/83

Each offer is conditional on the simultaneous settlement of the others.

TO:

Mal Dempsey & Associates Pty. Ltd. Trading as

MAL DEMPSEY
& ASSOCIATES

Professionals

REAL ESTATE AGENTS—Licensee: M. Dempsey J.P.
95 SCARBOROUGH BEACH RD., SCARBOROUGH
TELEPHONE 341 6611

As Agent for the Vendor(s)

Full name, address and occupation I/WE GUIDO JOHN RAINOLDI (BUILDER) AND JOHN GERALD RAINOLDI

BOTH OF 112 MILLCREST STREET, DOUBLEVIEW WA 6018

.... ("the Purchaser")

HEREBY OFFER TO PURCHASE (as joint tenants/tenants in common) the land described in the Schedule hereto and all improvements thereon ("the Property") with vacant possession unless otherwise provided in the Conditions together with the Chattels (if any) described in the Schedule at the price and on the other terms set out in the Schedule and subject to the Conditions.

SCHEDULE

(i) **Description of property:** The land situated at and known as ..... 209, 307/36 TENTH

... AVENUE, MAYLANDS, "INGLECREST"

being Portion of .. SWAN ...... Location .... and being Lot 33, 43

on Strata Plan XXXXXXXXXXXX .. 7348 .... and being the whole/part of the land in

Certificate of Title Volume .. 1546 ...... Folio 633, 643 ....

(ii) **Purchase Price:** $ 38,000 ..... of which $ 2,000 .... is allocated to chattels.

(iii) **Manner of Payment:** A deposit of $ 2,000 .... of which $ .... - ....

"REFER CLAUSE 6"

is paid herewith and $ .... shall be paid within..... - ..... days of acceptance.

The balance of the purchase price shall be paid on settlement.

(iv) **Settlement Date:** ..... ON OR BEFORE 30-4-1985

(v) **Chattels, including Plant & Equipment:** .... AS INSPECTED

....

....

....

CONDITIONS

Delete if not required by the Purchaser

1. (1.1) This Contract is conditional upon the undermentioned Lender(s), or any other lender(s) acceptable to the Purchaser, approving on or before the latest date for approval specified hereunder, the granting to the Purchaser of a loan(s) of an amount not less than the amount(s) specified.

(1.2) The Purchaser shall:-
   (a) use his best endeavours to obtain such loan(s)
   and
   (b) notify the Vendor or his Agent in writing of the approval (or otherwise) not later than forty-eight (48) hours after the latest date for approval.

(1.3) If the condition in paragraph (1.1) hereof shall not be fully satisfied by the latest date for approval then subject to the Purchaser having complied with paragraph (1.2) hereof UNLESS the Purchaser shall have waived this condition and communicated such waiver in writing to the Vendor or his Agent prior to the latest date for approval, then this Contract shall be deemed to have come to an end without the necessity for either party giving notice to that effect, whereupon the deposit and all other moneys (if any) paid hereunder shall forthwith be refunded to the Purchaser and there shall be no further claim under the Contract by either the Vendor or the Purchaser, against the other either at law or in equity.

(1.4) This clause shall operate for the benefit of both the Vendor and the Purchaser.

	First Mortgage	**Second Mortgage**
Lender:	)	
Latest Date for Approval:	) "REFER CLAUSE 7"	
Amount of Loan:	)	

Two more of the 17 properties being traded.

2. Acceptance of this offer shall be sufficiently communicated to the Purchaser if notification thereof shall be given by the Vendor's Agent to the Purchaser.

3. THE REAL ESTATE INSTITUTE OF WESTERN AUSTRALIA (Inc.) GENERAL CONDITIONS FOR THE SALE OF LAND (1982 REVISION) shall be incorporated herein and shall apply to this sale so far as they are not varied by or inconsistent with the express terms hereof.

(conditions as required to be added hereunder)

4. THIS OFFER IS SUBJECT TO THE VENDOR PURCHASING THE "STATION STREET SHOPPING CENTRE".

5. THE VENDOR AGREES ON THE PURCHASER TAKING POSSESSION ON THE 30TH APRIL 1983, ALL RENTS WILL GO TO THE PURCHASER AS DOES THE LIABILITIES OF ALL RATES, MAINTENANCE, MANAGEMENT FEES ETC.

6. THE DEPOSIT IS MADE UP OF PART EQUITY FROM THE STATION STREET SHOPPING CENTRE (IE. $2,000)

7. THE PURCHASER AGREES TO PAY 16% P.A. (INTEREST ONLY) ON THE AMOUNT OF $36,000 UNTIL SETTLEMENT.

8. THE VENDOR AGREES TO EXECUTE ANY CONTRACT OR TRANSFER NECESSARY, SHOULD THE PURCHASER WISH TO RE-SELL.

9. THE VENDOR AGREES TO CONTINUE THE PAYMENTS ON THE EXISTING MORTGAGES FOR THE PERIOD OF THIS CONTRACT.

Purchaser: .... Purchaser: ....

Witness: .... Witness: ....

Date: 19/4/83 Date: 19/4/83

I/WE   NANDI HOLDINGS (COOTAMUNDRA) PTY. LTD. AND

KANDEHA (HOLDINGS) PTY. LTD.

of   92 COOPER STREET, COOTAMUNDRA

("the Vendor") HEREBY ACCEPTS the above offer and acknowledges that the selling fee payable to the Vendor's Agent is my/our responsibility.

Vendor: KANDEHA (HOLDINGS) P/L   DIRECTOR   Vendor: N HOLDINGS (C'A) P/L   DIRECTOR

Witness: ....   Witness: ....

Date: 21/4/83 Date: 21/4/83

The parties respectively appoint the Solicitor or Settlement Agent named hereunder to act on their behalf in respect of this transaction and agree to pay their costs in respect thereto.

Name of Purchaser's Representative   Name of Vendor's Representative

....

Signature (Purchaser)   Signature (Vendor)

A true copy of this document has been received by each of the signatories hereto—together with a copy of THE REAL ESTATE INSTITUTE OF WESTERN AUSTRALIA (Inc.) GENERAL CONDITIONS FOR THE SALE OF LAND (1982 REVISION).

.... DATE 19/4/83 .... DATE 19/4/83

.... DATE 21/4/83 .... DATE 21/4/83

The same subject clauses as previous.

73

TO:

MAL DEMPSEY & ASSOCIATES

Professionals

REAL ESTATE AGENTS—Licensee: M. Dempsey J.P.
95 SCARBOROUGH BEACH RD., SCARBOROUGH
TELEPHONE 341 6611

Mal Dempsey & Associates Pty. Ltd. Trading as

As Agent for the Vendor(s)

Full name, address and occupation I/WE .... GUIDO JOHN RAINOLDI (BUILDER) AND JOHN GERALD RAINOLDI (BUILDER) ...

.... BOTH OF 112 MILLCREST STREET, DOUBLEVIEW WA 6018 ....

.... ("the Purchaser")

HEREBY OFFER TO PURCHASE (as joint tenants/tenants in common) the land described in the Schedule hereto and all improvements thereon ("the Property") with vacant possession unless otherwise provided in the Conditions together with the Chattels (if any) described in the Schedule at the price and on the other terms set out in the Schedule and subject to the Conditions.

SCHEDULE

(i) **Description of property:** The land situated at and known as .. A6, B21, C6, C8, C12, ..

.. C15, 16, C17, C18, C23, C24/305 HARBORNE STREET, GLENDALOUGH ..

....

being Portion of .... Location .... and being Lot ....

on Strata Plan/Plan/Diagram .... and being the whole/part of the land in

Certificate of Title Volume .... Folio ....

(ii) **Purchase Price:** $ 253,000 .... of which $ 22,000 .... is allocated to chattels.

(iii) **Manner of Payment:** A deposit of $ 19,000 .... of which $. —
"REFER CLAUSE 6"
is paid herewith and $ .... shall be paid within ..... — .... days of acceptance.

The balance of the purchase price shall be paid on settlement.

(iv) **Settlement Date:** ON OR BEFORE 30-4-1985 ....

(v) **Chattels, including Plant & Equipment:** NIL ....

....

....

....

CONDITIONS

Delete if not required by the Purchaser

1. (1.1) This Contract is conditional upon the undermentioned Lender(s), or any other lender(s) acceptable to the Purchaser, approving on or before the latest date for approval specified hereunder, the granting to the Purchaser of a loan(s) of an amount not less than the amount(s) specified.
   (1.2) The Purchaser shall—
   (a) use his best endeavours to obtain such loan(s)
   and
   (b) notify the Vendor or his Agent in writing of the approval (or otherwise) not later than forty-eight (48) hours after the latest date for approval.
   (1.3) If the condition in paragraph (1.1) hereof shall not be fully satisfied by the latest date for approval then subject to the Purchaser having complied with paragraph (1.2) hereof UNLESS the Purchaser shall have waived this condition and communicated such waiver in writing to the Vendor or his Agent prior to the latest date for approval, then this Contract shall be deemed to have come to an end without the necessity for either party giving notice to that effect, whereupon the deposit and all other moneys (if any) paid hereunder shall forthwith be refunded to the Purchaser and there shall be no further claim under the Contract by either the Vendor or the Purchaser against the other either at law or in equity.
   (1.4) This clause shall operate for the benefit of both the Vendor and the Purchaser.

	First Mortgage	Second Mortgage
Lender:	)	
Latest Date for Approval:	) "REFER CLAUSE 7"	
Amount of Loan:	)	

Eleven of the properties being traded.

2. Acceptance of this offer shall be sufficiently communicated to the Purchaser if notification thereof shall be given by the Vendor's Agent to the Purchaser.

3. THE REAL ESTATE INSTITUTE OF WESTERN AUSTRALIA (Inc.) GENERAL CONDITIONS FOR THE SALE OF LAND (1982 REVISION) shall be incorporated herein and shall apply to this sale so far as they are not varied by or inconsistent with the express terms hereof.

(conditions as required to be added hereunder)

4. THIS OFFER IS SUBJECT TO THE VENDOR PURCHASING "THE STATION STREET SHOPPING CENTRE"

5. THE VENDOR AGREES, ON THE PURCHASER TAKING POSSESSION ON THE 30TH APRIL 1983, ALL RENTS WILL GO TO THE PURCHASER AS DOES THE LIABILITIES OF ALL RATES, MAINTENANCE, MANAGEMENT FEES ETC.

6. THE DEPOSIT OF $19,000 IS MADE UP OF PART EQUITY FROM THE STATION STREET SHOPPING CENTRE.

7. THE PURCHASER TAKES OVER THEIR OWN MORTGAGES UPON POSSESSION.

8. THE VENDORS AGREE TO EXECUTE ANY CONTRACTS OR TRANSFERS NECESSARY, SHOULD THE PURCHASER SELL ANY OR ALL OF THE MENTIONED PROPERTIES.

Purchaser: .... Purchaser: ....
Witness: .... Witness: ....
Date: 19/4/83 Date: 19/4/83

I/WE NANDI HOLDINGS (COOTAMUNDRA) PTY. LTD. AND KANDEHA (HOLDINGS) PTY. LTD.

of 92 COOPER STREET, COOTAMUNDRA

("the Vendor") HEREBY ACCEPTS the above offer and acknowledges that the selling fee payable to the Vendor's Agent is my/our responsibility.

Vendor: .... Vendor: ....
Witness: .... Witness: ....
Date: 21/4/83 Date: 21/4/83

The parties respectively appoint the Solicitor or Settlement Agent named hereunder to act on their behalf in respect of this transaction and agree to pay their costs in respect thereto.

Name of Purchaser's Representative   Name of Vendor's Representative

Signature (Purchaser)   Signature (Vendor)

A true copy of this document has been received by each of the signatories hereto—together with a copy of THE REAL ESTATE INSTITUTE OF WESTERN AUSTRALIA (Inc.) GENERAL CONDITIONS FOR THE SALE OF LAND (1982 REVISION)

.... DATE 19/4/83 .... DATE 19/4/83
.... DATE 21/4/83 .... DATE 21/4/8

This concludes the 17 trades on the shopping centre. That's 18 sales in all.
I again re-listed the 17 trades as the Rinaldi family did not want to keep them.
I sold all 17 in the next three months, full commission received again.
LIST and LAST.

11

Marketing Property

The marketing effort that went into getting the listing is one thing; now you have to market the property.

- Has the commercial property environment changed?
- Has the residential property environment changed?
- Have prices changed?
- Have returns changed?
- Have tax rates changed?
- Have interest rates changed?
- What is the impact of the GST?

A bigger question: Can commercial and industrial property be marketed in the same way as residential property? Yes, and the possibilities are even wider.

Why So Many Failed

The failure of many commercial and industrial representatives stems from the fact that they had life far too easy for far too long. In the 1970s and 1980s huge volumes of sales were taking place with large insurance companies, banks and superannuation funds. In the 1980s and 1990s property trusts, both listed and unlisted, came to the fore and joined the other major players.

A commercial or industrial firms would list a shopping centre or office block, produce a copy of the rent schedule (in most cases they were the managing agents) and capitalise the rental return at perhaps 10 per cent net return. So if the net rent amounted to $100,000 per annum, for example, the price would be $1,000,000. And then followed the question 'Who shall we put this one to?'.

In earlier days interest rates were 10 to 13 per cent fixed for three years. This made for quite an easy presentation, especially if there was a blue-chip tenant and reasonably solid minor tenants. If a purchaser was putting in say 20 per cent deposit and the net return was 10 per cent on the purchase price, the scenario would look something like this:

Property price	1,000,000
10% net return	100,000
$800,000 mortgage at 12% interest	96,000
Annual surplus	$4,000

This had to be too easy.

Dealing with Change

Where have our blue-chip companies gone? Marketing of commercial and industrial real estate has surely changed, but are we keeping abreast of it? If we think for a second, we'll realise that the entire world has changed.

How many clients have told you they have $1,000,000 sitting in the bank just waiting for you to sell them real estate? In my experience there are some, but they are very few. Let's take the aforementioned shopping centre and have it strata titled into say ten shops. They will vary in price depending on position and size, but for this exercise we'll say they are the same.

With normal lending of 80 per cent we would be looking for ten people with $20,000 each to invest. How about getting the vendor to carry a 10 per cent second mortgage? Suddenly I am looking for ten people with as little as $10,000 as deposit or only five prepared to put up $20,000. Smaller investors find this market very attractive. I have done this exercise successfully with Padbury Medical Centre, Burrendah House Shopping Centre, Gosnells Medical Centre, Heathridge Shopping Centre, Maddington Commercial Centre, Station Street Shopping Centre and Erindale Commercial Centre Balcatta W.A.

> The Heathridge Shopping Centre had been listed for $1,300,000. After strata titling we disposed of all Stage One shops, with the exception of one that had already been sold, to clients from New South Wales. All deals were done through a single firm of accountants within ten days in March 1982. The same shopping centre could have been advertised for twelve to eighteen months at $1,300,000 and still not sold.

> Once again, a complete marketing package had been put together. We had finance available at up to 95 per cent gearing (first mortgage to 85 per cent, second to 95 per cent by vendor, i.e. 10 per cent second mortgage). To purchase the biggest shop – the $200,000 supermarket – a deposit of only $10,000 (5 per cent of $200,000) was needed.

We all have lots of clients with $10,000 or $20,000 to invest – not necessarily cash; don't forget their equity – but very few with $1,300,000. The smaller shops in this complex sold for as little as $88,000, meaning only $8,800 was required as a deposit if we were talking 10 per cent and as little as $4,400 on 5 per cent.

For the vacant shops we were able to offer an assured net return of 10 per cent on the purchase price, this figure having been guaranteed for the first two years, or until let, by the developers/vendors. This undertaking on their part paid off when all units sold quickly.

Highest and Best Use

With valuations there is always talk of the 'highest and best use'. Why don't we apply this same terminology to marketing? We

Heathridge Shopping Centre

should look at every property and see if we can find that 'other market'. In many instances the best solution can be strata titling, the result normally being that the vendor will receive a higher aggregate price as well as a speedier sale – ten individual purchasers will pay a higher price than an institution buying the whole property. Not to be overlooked is the fact that the commissions for your firm and yourself are that much better also under such an arrangement. Let us look again at the case of the Heathridge Shopping Centre.

A $1,300,000 sale would have generated a commission of $27,720, but the actual figures break down as follows:

Price of unit	Commission
$200,000	$5,720
$ 88,000	$3,265
$ 96,000	$3,485
$ 98,000	$3,540
$110,000	$3,820
$120,000	$4,045
$138,000	$4,450
3 x $150,000	$14,160

Total sales price 1.3m.
All properties sold for full asking price.

Thus the total commission was $42,485, a margin of $14,765 – or more than 50 per cent – over what would have been payable if the whole complex had been sold in one transaction.

We always offer first purchase opportunity to the tenant. Probably none of them could look at buying the entire centre, but there is every chance they could afford to buy their individual shop. Even where they don't follow through, the approach will keep the tenants on side because you gave them the first opportunity.

If a tenant has a good equity in their home, they normally would be able to utilise this to purchase the shop using equity borrowings. It is very important to look at the purchaser's current structure when considering whose name should be on the title. Is it a partnership, a company or a family trust? If it is a husband-and-wife team, do they operate as a partnership? Is their income the same? The fact that their family home is in joint names as joint tenants does not mean that the same should necessarily apply to the investment purchase. Look at the tax implications.

Factory Units

With factory units the same generally applies as for shopping centres. The option of design to the compliance of strata titling prior to construction has much to be said for it – even though, as often happens, the entire development might go to one owner. In cases where things turn out that way, single owners have a great deal of flexibility: they are able to sell a unit, or several of them, if they ever need money; if they need to borrow funds for their initial purchase, they can allocate three or four units to be mortgaged and keep the balance unencumbered. Never make available more security to a lender than is needed: it is amazing how hard it can be to get them to release some if you would like to see it applied to another purpose at a later date.

What size should factory units be? Best to have a mix of sizes, e.g. 2 x 100 m², 2 x 200 m², 2 x 250 m². This will suit the small owner-occupier. With this configuration, sizes of 300 m², 400 m² and 500 m² are also available. Always have flexibility.

Office Units

With office units also it's a case of looking at all avenues and bringing the concept to a majority market.

- How little deposit does a client need?
- What trading will take place there?
- Can you get the tenant to purchase the property?
  - Can you make it an attractive proposition?
  - Does the vendor really need all the proceeds?

- What is the vendor going to do with the money?
- Did the vendor buy prior to the introduction of capital gains tax?
- Have you covered a possible contract of sale?

- Avoid advertising – do you really want to give 50 per cent of your commission to another agent?

One example was Kobolt House in West Perth.

PROPERTY INVESTMENT IS WITHIN THE MEANS OF MR/MS AVERAGE

The architect's perspective showed the completed office complex in Prowse Street, West Perth, which was sold in 1982 as strata-titled office suites by our real estate firm. There were only a few left. The new owners had retain the company to manage their suites. One of the main features was common secretarial and reception facilities and access to a common boardroom on each floor. Prices range from $55,500, while the penthouse was priced at $300,000.
The building's spectacular, yet functional design and prime location in West Perth, make this type of investment a key asset in any property portfolio.

Motels/Hotels

Normally a town has at least one motel or hotel. In cities there are many. Why do we always regard these buildings as a single entity? Bear this in mind: even international luxury hotel chains do not in most cases own the buildings that can be found with their names emblazoned across them around the world. They lease them.

We are all screaming out for stock to sell, no matter where we are situated, and too often we can't see what is before our very eyes. Most hotels and motels are on one title, just like the old blocks of flats, but is there any need for this to be so? I could give numerous examples of hotels and motels – as well as blocks of flats/home units, factories, offices and shopping centres – that have been approved for strata title over the last thirty years. We have proposed/coordinated a number of these projects in Mandurah, Perth and Scarborough.

We sold forty-three units in a Scarborough development in a three-month period in 1988. Each unit was priced at $80,000 with a deposit of $12,000. The first mortgage of $68,000 was supplied by the vendor at 13.5 per cent for a period of three years. The units were leased to a national operator under an arrangement by which the purchaser received $104 per week whether they were occupied or not.

West Beach Lagoon, Scarborough

The operator paid all shire and water rates and most of the maintenance. The property was leased for a five-year period with three more five-year options. These units come up from time to time for re-sale. There was also a second block of twelve units, again on a separate strata title.

From the operator's point of view, there is not the burden of outlaying capital to buy freehold property, yet the twenty-year lease offers excellent security. From the individual strata owner's point of view, there is no concern that the tenant might leave after six months.

Strata titling such properties can provide real estate agents with additional sources of stock.

The Mount Street Inn in Perth had been a four-star hotel. It was converted to strata-titled serviced apartments with a full hotel licence and the normal facilitiesof a hotel on the ground floor. Features include a gym, undercover car parking, full reception, a restaurant, bars and a function centre.

The Mount Street Inn, Perth CBD

Just over a hundred strata-titled units were created, the majority being the former hotel rooms. To meet City of Perth requirements, all the units had to be self-contained – each already had a bathroom, but now they had to have a mini kitchen installed. This was achieved by creating a small cupboard with two hot plates, a microwave oven and an electric frying pan.

There were five or six different layouts, varying from single bed, twin share and suites through to family units. The price for each was based on unit entitlement and ranged from $106,000 to $180,000. The developers offered vendor's terms of 20 per cent deposit and 15 per cent, interest only, for three years.

The vendors offered 8 per cent per annum net rental return on purchase price for the first year, increasing to 9 per cent for the second year, after which the rate would float with the market.

Holding Up a Mirror

Now let's look at marketing a vacant land subdivision in a sick economy. Selling is an art, and we must be creative. In this case we have an investor developer who can't sell his land. Could we find a buyer by advertising it? Probably not. But might we be able to find a way of making the property look attractive to someone who doesn't want to buy land? Let's find a builder who has some office units that aren't moving. Can we marry the two?

Show the builder how he can get on and build specs on the vacant land rather than sit in limbo awaiting the sale of the office units. Remind the investor developer that his vacant land is showing him no return, whereas he is up for rates and land tax, and the lack of income means he can't negative gear. The way I often put it is: *Ants don't pay rent.* However, if he were to exchange his vacant land for some units in an office building, this would bring benefit to both parties.

Marketing is all about *mirrors*. When looking in a mirror, we want to see the best reflection. The same goes with listings – they are reflected by sales.

> I had two clients, one with vacant Marangaroo land that had been subdivided into residential lots, the other with office units in West Perth (Kolbolt House). Both wanted to sell for whatever reason. 'The grass is always greener', so it was a case of formulating some options. We had four strata-titled office units, currently vacant, but so was the land. It's impossible to rent out vacant residential lots, but the owners were able to see that, if they had the offices instead, they would have the option to let and hold until the market picked up, then sell if they wished. And there was the all-important negative gearing aspect.

> The builder realised that, if he owned the residential lots rather than the office units, he would be able to get back to work. We arranged for each party to buy the other's properties.

> The builder developed most of the lots and we sold a couple of others as vacant blocks. We naturally received full commission on the four offices and the nine residential lots from the appropriate vendors. The reflection in the mirror worked very well for all parties, including us. Trading is still alive and well!

Kobold House, Prowse Street, West Perth

(For Stamp Office Use Only.)

 TO:

MAL DEMPSEY
Professionals

REAL ESTATE AGENTS—Licensee: M. Dempsey J.P.
95 SCARBOROUGH BEACH RD., SCARBOROUGH
TELEPHONE 341 6611

As Agent for the Vendor(s)

Full name, address and occupation

I/WE   A & M Nominees Pty Ltd AS TRUSTEES FOR THE A & M UNIT TRUST

OF 193 MAIN STREET OSBORNE PARK WA 6017

.... ("the Purchaser")

HEREBY OFFER TO PURCHASE (as joint tenants/tenants in common) the land described in the Schedule hereto and all improvements thereon ("the Property") with vacant possession unless otherwise provided in the Conditions together with the Chattels (if any) described in the Schedule at the price and on the other terms set out in the Schedule and subject to the Conditions.

SCHEDULE

(i) Description of property: The land situated at and known as Units 1,2,3 & 8/17

PROWSE STREET WEST PERTH ....

....

being Portion of Perth town Location V137,138 and being Lot 1,2,3,8

xxxxxxxxxxxxxxx/Diagram 10552 and being the whole/part of the land in

Certificate of Title Volume 1623 Folio 101,102,103,108

(ii) Purchase Price: $ 195,750 of which $ 5,750 is allocated to chattels.

(iii) Manner of Payment: A deposit of $ at NIL of which $ NIL

is paid herewith and $ 195,750 shall be ~~paid within~~ .... ~~days of acceptance.~~

The balance of the purchase price shall be paid on settlement.

(iv) Settlement Date: on or before 3/4/1984 ....

(v) Chattels, including Plant & Equipment: CARPETS ....

....

....

....

CONDITIONS

1. (1.1) This Contract is conditional upon the undermentioned Lender(s), or any other lender(s) acceptable to the Purchaser, approving on or before the latest date for approval specified hereunder, the granting to the Purchaser of a loan(s) of an amount not less than the amount(s) specified.
   (1.2) The Purchaser shall—
   (a) use his best endeavours to obtain such loan(s)
   and
   (b) notify the Vendor or his Agent in writing of the approval (or otherwise) not later than forty-eight (48) hours after the latest date for approval.
   (1.3) If the condition in paragraph (1.1) hereof shall not be fully satisfied by the latest date for approval then subject to the Purchaser having complied with paragraph (1.2) hereof UNLESS the Purchaser shall have waived this condition and communicated such waiver in writing to the Vendor or his Agent prior to the latest date for approval, then this Contract shall be deemed to have come to an end without the necessity for either party giving notice to that effect, whereupon the deposit and all other moneys (if any) paid hereunder shall forthwith be refunded to the Purchaser and there shall be no further claim under the Contract by either the Vendor or the Purchaser against the other either at law or in equity.
   (1.4) This clause shall operate for the benefit of both the Vendor and the Purchaser.

	First Mortgage	Second Mortgage
	CASH AT SETTLEMENT	
Lender:		
Latest Date for Approval:		
Amount of Loan:		

Delete if not required by the Purchaser

Mirrors - The purchaser here saw more merit selling their offices to acquire 10 blocks of land.

2. Acceptance of this offer shall be sufficiently communicated to the Purchaser if notification thereof shall be given by the Vendor's Agent to the Purchaser.

3. The ~~Law Society of Western Australia (Inc.) and~~ The Real Estate Institute of Western Australia (Inc.) ~~1984 JOINT FORM OF~~ GENERAL CONDITIONS FOR THE SALE OF LAND shall be incorporated herein and shall apply to this sale so far as they are not varied by or inconsistent with the express terms hereof.

(conditions as required to be added hereunder)

Subject to the vendor purchasing Lots 815,816,817,813 SHORNE PLACE LOT 809,812,802 ADDINGTON

WAY LOT 844 LOT 7755 WANLEY STREET LOT 680 BREDGAR WAY

SUBJECT TO THE VENDOR GUARANTEEING A 12% GROSS RETURN PER ANNUM FOR A PERIOD OF TWO YEARS

for and on behalf of GUSS PTY LTD

Purchaser: *Hostii*   Purchaser:

Witness: *Klinsman*   Witness:

Date: *3/3/1965*   Date:

I/WE *MAC DEMPSEY & ASSOCIATES*

of *95 SCARBOROUGH BEACH ROAD, SCARBOROUGH*

("the Vendor") HEREBY ACCEPTS the above offer and acknowledges that the selling fee payable to the Vendor's Agent is my/our responsibility.

Vendor: *W Dempsey John*   Vendor:

Witness: *signed*   Witness:

Date: *5/3/1985*   Date:

The parties respectively appoint the Solicitor or Settlement Agent named hereunder to act on their behalf in respect of this transaction and agree to pay their costs in respect thereto.

Name of Purchaser's Representative   Name of Vendor's Representative

CONVEYANCING AND SETTLEMENT SERVICES   *MAC SMITHSON*

Hostii   *signed*

Signature (Purchaser)   Signature (Vendor)

A true copy of this document has been received by each of the signatories hereto – together with a copy of The ~~Law Society of Western Australia (Inc.) and~~ The Real Estate Institute of Western Australia (Inc.) ~~1984 JOINT FORM OF~~ GENERAL CONDITIONS FOR THE SALE OF LAND.

Hostii   DATE *3/85*   DATE / /

W Dempsey   DATE *5/3/85*   DATE / /

signed   DATE *5/3/85*   DATE / /

Each offer is subject to the simultaneous settlement of the other.

approved by
**THE REAL ESTATE INSTITUTE OF
WESTERN AUSTRALIA (INC.)
AND
THE SETTLEMENT AGENTS
ASSOCIATION (INC.)
1982 REVISION — COPYRIGHT**

(For Stamp Office Use Only.)

TO: Mal Dempsey & Associates Pty Ltd, trading as

MAL DEMPSEY
Professionals

REAL ESTATE AGENTS—Licensee: M. Dempsey J.P.
95 SCARBOROUGH BEACH RD., SCARBOROUGH
TELEPHONE 341 6611

As Agent for the Vendor(s)

Full name, address and occupation

I/WE Guido John Rainoldi (Builder) and John Gerrald Rainoldi (Builder)

BOTH OF 112 MILLCREST STREET DOUBLEVIEW

.... ("the Purchaser")

HEREBY OFFER TO PURCHASE (as joint tenants/tenants in common) the land described in the Schedule hereto and all improvements thereon ("the Property") with vacant possession unless otherwise provided in the Conditions together with the Chattels (if any) described in the Schedule at the price and on the other terms set out in the Schedule and subject to the Conditions.

SCHEDULE

(i) Description of property: The land situated at and known as ....

LOT 815,816,817,813 SHORNE PLACE LOT 809,812,802 ADDINGTON WAY

LOT LOT 844 LOT 7755 WANLEY STREET LOT 680 BREDGAR WAY

being Portion of .... Location .... and being Lot ....

XXXXXXXXXXXXXXX/Diagram .... and being the whole/part of the land in

Certificate of Title Volume .... Folio ....

(ii) Purchase Price: $ 217,800 of which $ NIL .... is allocated to chattels.

(iii) Manner of Payment: A deposit of $ NIL .... of which $ NIL ....

is paid herewith and $ .... shall be paid within .... days of acceptance.

The balance of the purchase price shall be paid on settlement.

(iv) Settlement Date: ....

(v) Chattels, including Plant & Equipment: ....
NIL

....

....

CONDITIONS

1. (1.1) This Contract is conditional upon the undermentioned Lender(s), or any other lender(s) acceptable to the Purchaser, approving on or before the latest date for approval specified hereunder, the granting to the Purchaser of a loan(s) of an amount not less than the amount(s) specified.
   (1.2) The Purchaser shall:—
      (a) use his best endeavours to obtain such loan(s)
         and
      (b) notify the Vendor or his Agent in writing of the approval (or otherwise) not later than forty-eight (48) hours after the latest date for approval.
   (1.3) If the condition in paragraph (1.1) hereof shall not be fully satisfied by the latest date for approval then subject to the Purchaser having complied with paragraph (1.2) hereof UNLESS the Purchaser shall have waived this condition and communicated such waiver in writing to the Vendor or his Agent prior to the latest date for approval, then this Contract shall be deemed to have come to an end without the necessity for either party giving notice to that effect, whereupon the deposit and all other moneys (if any) paid hereunder shall forthwith be refunded to the Purchaser and there shall be no further claim under the Contract by either the Vendor or the Purchaser against the other either at law or in equity.
   (1.4) This clause shall operate for the benefit of both the Vendor and the Purchaser.

Delete if not required by the Purchaser

	First Mortgage	Second Mortgage
	BANK OR FINANCE COMPANY	
Lender:		
Latest Date for Approval:	16/3/84	
	AS REQUIRED	

The offer and acceptance on the ten blocks of land traded on the four office units.

2. Acceptance of this offer shall be sufficiently communicated to the Purchaser if notification thereof shall be given by the Vendor's Agent to the Purchaser.

3. The Law Society of Western Australia (Inc.) and The Real Estate Institute of Western Australia (Inc.) 1982 JOINT FORM OF GENERAL CONDITIONS FOR THE SALE OF LAND shall be incorporated herein and shall apply to this sale so far as they are not varied by or inconsistent with the express terms hereof.

conditions as required to be added hereunder)

SUBJECT TO THE VENDOR PURCHASING UNITS 1,2,3,8/17 PROWSE STREET WEST PERTH

for and on behalf of GUSS PTY LTD

Purchaser: _____ Purchaser: _____

Witness: _____ Witness: _____

Date: 3/3/1985 Date: _____

I/WE MAC DEMPSEY & ASSOCIATES

of 95 SCARBOROUGH BEACH ROAD, SCARBOROUGH

("the Vendor") HEREBY ACCEPTS the above offer and acknowledges that the selling fee payable to the Vendor's Agent is my/our responsibility.

Vendor: _____ Vendor: _____

Witness: _____ Witness: _____

Date: 5/3/1985 Date: _____

The parties respectively appoint the Solicitor or Settlement Agent named hereunder to act on their behalf in respect of this transaction and agree to pay their costs in respect thereto.

Name of Purchaser's Representative   Name of Vendor's Representative

CONVEYANCING AND SETTLEMENT SERVICES   MAC SMITHSON

_____ _____
Signature (Purchaser)   Signature (Vendor)

A true copy of this document has been received by each of the signatories hereto – together with a copy of THE LAW SOCIETY WESTERN AUSTRALIA The Real Estate Institute of Western Australia (Inc.) 1982 JOINT FORM OF GENERAL CONDITIONS FOR THE SALE OF LAND.

_____ DATE 3/85 _____ DATE / /
_____ DATE 5.3.85 _____ DATE / /
_____ DATE 5.3.85 _____ DATE / /

> Luck? Make your own - The harder I work the luckier I get. This created 14 more sales. The moral of the story 'Be Different, Be Creative'.

Selling by Tender

Selling by tender is an alternative to auction or private treaty. When should we sell by tender?

We recommended that the premises of the International Brick Company, on 21.98 hectares of land fronting Beach Road and Alexander Drive, Malaga, be put to tender. We were competing with international commercial and industrial companies to get the appointment. How did we get it?

With our submission we appraised the value of sand. Eighty per cent of the site was a large hill of yellow sand with growth over the top. Every one of the firms we were competing against saw the hill as a problem that had to be dealt with, and were factoring in the cost of flattening the site.

The property sold by tender for $5.8 million. The successful tenderer allowed $650,000 for the sale of the sand. The first three tenderers allowed value for the sand on our recommendation. Taking into account one agent's estimate that it would cost about $350,000 to get rid of the sand, our strategy probably lifted the price by about $1 million.

Be creative – be different. But remember, not every property should be put to tender.

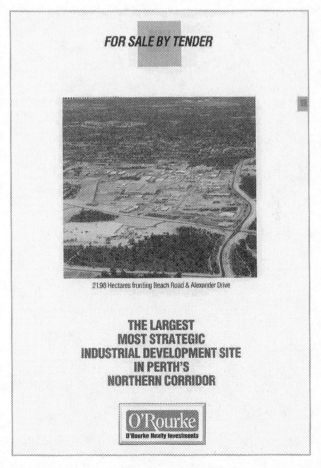

FOR SALE BY TENDER

21.98 Hectares fronting Beach Road & Alexander Drive

THE LARGEST
MOST STRATEGIC
INDUSTRIAL DEVELOPMENT SITE
IN PERTH'S
NORTHERN CORRIDOR

O'Rourke
O'Rourke Realty Investments

12

More on Selling Residential Property for Investment

The biggest cost in running a sales team is advertising. Why do we advertise? Is it to pacify your vendor? When you do advertise, do you stay in the office or at home to take the calls? Do you answer your mobile telephones when it rings? If not, why did you advertise? Even if we are very careful about such matters, there is always the question of whether advertising is the best way of marketing a particular property.

Know Your Subjects – Think Outside the Square

- finance (all options)
- deposits (where do they come from?)
- VTDI Form 221D of the Tax Act
- GST and its role
- Strata Titles Act
- capital gains rules
- capital losses
- CCH updates
- foreign investment
- prepayment of interest

If you do not have an investment co-ordinator in your office, you need to know all of this.

Knowledge is Power

✓ Wealth Building
✓ Tax Planning
✓ Health
✓ Happiness
✓ Common Sense
✓ Learn from mistakes

The middle two are the most important. All the money in the world won't give you health or happiness.
To be really creative you have to enjoy what you are doing.

O'Rourke

Analyse Your Market

Why compete with every other estate agent? I say it again: Be different and be creative. While you look for people who want to buy real estate, every other agent in Australia is doing the same.

Instead, I am looking for people who pay too much tax and, believe me, I have never found a person who doesn't pay enough. If this is true, everyone is a prospect for my gearing exercises. What do we mean by gearing? The term is commonly understood in the real estate industry, but let's go over it. By gearing we mean controlling a large investment with a small amount of money. This is done by borrowing or mortgaging. The owner, and not the man who holds the mortgage, stands to gain in the rising market presently anticipated. The following example will illustrate the point:

A and B own identical rental buildings each worth $180,000. A has a clear title while B has a $120,000 mortgage. If the value of each building increases by 33.33 per cent, A has increased his equity by that proportion – from $180,000 to $240,000 – but B's equity has soared 100 per cent – from $60,000 to $120,000. In addition, A has to pay tax on his rental income as he has only minimum deductions – rates, land tax, management fees, strata fees, etc. – while B claims the shortfall between her rental income and her expenses, which include all the interest she pays on the mortgage.

If A had purchased five properties and mortgaged each, instead of holding a clear title, his rise in equity would have been five times as great with the same initial investment.

> My parents brought us up like Client A in the example. We brought our children up like Client B. There's a huge difference.

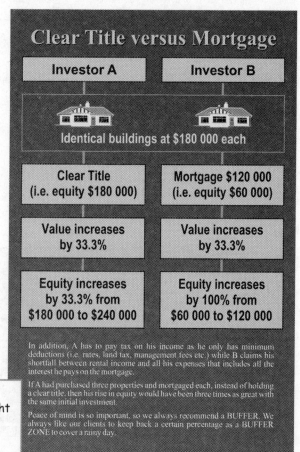

Clear Title versus Mortgage

Investor A	Investor B
Identical buildings at $180 000 each	
Clear Title (i.e. equity $180 000)	Mortgage $120 000 (i.e. equity $60 000)
Value increases by 33.3%	Value increases by 33.3%
Equity increases by 33.3% from $180 000 to $240 000	Equity increases by 100% from $60 000 to $120 000

In addition, A has to pay tax on his income as he only has minimum deductions (i.e. rates, land tax, management fees etc.) while B claims his shortfall between rental income and all his expenses that includes all the interest he pays on the mortgage.

If A had purchased three properties and mortgaged each, instead of holding a clear title, then his rise in equity would have been three times as great with the same initial investment.

Peace of mind is so important, so we always recommend a BUFFER. We always like our clients to keep back a certain percentage as a BUFFER ZONE to cover a rainy day.

Ups and Downs

It is generally accepted that real estate has grown in value by an average of 9 per cent per annum over 1200 years in Britain and by 12% over 100 years in Australia. While that is the sort of growth we anticipate when we buy real estate for investment, there is no guarantee that will be the situation every year. Peace of mind is important, so we always recommend a 'buffer' to cover for the rainy day that might come along.

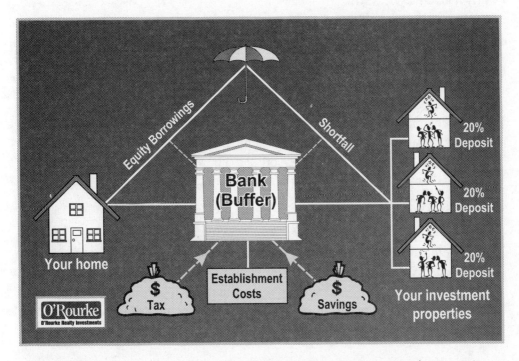

We originally paid a deposit on our loans, as the years went on we gained more equity in our homes, mainly through Real Estate going up, rather than the capital we paid off. As your property rises in value you can borrow against your new found equity to purchase additional properties.

By borrowing enough to cover the deposits on each of the proposed purchases, say 20% on each, also borrowing enough to cover the establishment costs, stamp duty, settlement fees, legal costs, bank fees etc. Borrow enough to cover the short fall, working on say 48 weeks a year for say two years.

Will your own property still go up in value, will each of the properties purchased go up in value? YES

Any additional funds you earn, put back into your buffer account. Any tax refunds, put back into your buffer account. Best example is an Equity Facility. You only pay interest if you are using the money.

This becomes our umbrella for a rainy day. This takes the risk out of borrowing. You are always working in your own comfort zone.

Peace of mind is so important.

The principle here is to have a statutory reserve, just like the banks. Yes, follow their example – they borrow, borrow, borrow! The best approach is through use of an equity facility. Such a facility, used as a buffer, takes the risk out of the investment, and we only pay interest when we use the money. If we don't need to use it, basically there is no charge.

Why Not Pay Cash?

In my earlier days in the business, people would come to me wanting to pay cash for a duplex half. I would spend hours showing them that the return on residential properties was 4 to 6 per cent gross, which is useless in today's world. But, if they were to purchase both units, putting 40 per cent deposit on each, they would avoid paying tax because this is imposed only on the net income, not the gross. By the time they paid all the normal outgoings, plus interest on the mortgages, they would break even or show a slight loss. However both properties would go up in value, so they would be gaining capital wealth. As they had used only 80 per cent of their money, they would have enough to cover all other contingencies and any possible shortfall.

Tax Benefits

If you are fortunate enough to show a loss, then this is a tax deduction against your other income. We have sold hundreds of Perth properties to local and eastern states clients. The majority of these sales have come about through the work of our Investment Division, which specialises in 'gearing and leverage'. The purchasers in the main have been geared for taxation deductions and capital wealth – in that order.

Why Perth Property?

Eastern states clients can buy two or three properties in Perth for every one they can buy in Sydney or the Gold Coast (and of course it's the same tax Australia-wide). While we continue to deal with the public and our existing clients, more recently we have been working with accountants and financial advisers who are putting taxation packages together for themselves and their clients. I have sold some four hundred properties through just one New South Wales firm of accountants, whose clients are buying real estate for the purpose of securing tax deductions.

The History of Perth Residential Real Estate

For many years it has been said that your best investment is your own home. But is it really? – from the following table it obviously depends upon where you purchase.

This table shows the healthy increase in property prices between 1961 and 2001.

Hindsight – As the value of your own home went up could you have taken equity out and bought a 2nd or 3rd property. Hindsight is a wonderful thing.

Suburb	1961 ($)	1981 ($)	1961-1981 increase	Annual increase	June 2001 ($)	1981-2001 increase	Annual increase
Applecross	13 000	91 000	700%	35.0% p.a.	501 400	551%	27.5% p.a.
City Beach	17 000	120 000	700%	35% p.a.	607 000	506%	25.3% p.a.
Dalkeith	13 000	200 000	1538%	76.0% p.a.	726 100	388%	19.4% p.a.
Floreat	12 000	90 000	750%	37.5% p.a.	386 300	429%	21.5% p.a.
North Perth	12 000	47 000	390%	19.5% p.a.	274 300	584%	29.2% p.a.
Scarborough	8 000	48 000	600%	30.0 p.a.	242 400	505%	25.2% p.a.

O'Rourke
O'Rourke Realty Investments

95

The use of Gearing in real estate - 1984 Three Clients with $30,000

Clients (A) 'Old School' pays cash for property
(B) Medium gearing (Tax savings)
(C) Person in high tax bracket (large tax savings)

Client (A) buys one unit for cash 28,500
Establishment cost 1,500
$30,000

Income   Rental $43.00 per week x 52 =   2,236
Less tax   750
$1,486

Annual expenses
Management fees   190.00
Shire rates   82.00
Water rates   68.00
Body corporate   144.00
Land tax   50.00
$534.00

> Net profit added to the top of your taxable income.

Capital gains @ 15% p.a. – *Based on history of 17% p.a. over 20 years.*

Purchase price $28,500

1st year	4,275	4th year	6,511
	32,775		49,856
2nd year	4,916	5th year	7,478
	37,691		57,334
3rd year	5,654		
	43,345	**Capital gain $ 28,834**	

Client (B) buys two units on terms

Purchase price	$45,000	$45,000
Deposit	9,000	9,000
Est, costs	1,500	1,500
Initial costs	$10,500	$10,500
Total deposit	18,000	
Total Est costs	3,000	
Reserve bank account buffer	9,000	
	$30,000	

Borrowed funds
36,000 @ 17% interest only $6,120 x 2 .... $12,240

Other expenses
Management fees 8.5%   255.00
Shire rates   157.00
Water rates   190.00
Body corporate   140.00
Land tax   58.00
$810.00 x 2   1,620
$13,860

Less income

Rental $60 per week x 52 = 3,120 x 2 =	6,240	
Nett loss	(7,620) **Tax deductible**	

Capital gain @ 15% p.a.– *Based on history of 17% p.a. over 20 years*

Purchase price $90,000

1st year 13,500	4th year 20,531
$103,500	$157,409
2nd year 15,525	5th year 23,610
$119,025	$181,019
3rd year 17,853	
$136,878	**Capital gain over 5 years $91,019**

> 1st year loss reduces your normal taxable income.

Client (C) buys three units on terms

Purchase price	$45,000	$46,000	$32,000
Deposit	9,000	9,200	6,400
Est. costs	1,500	1,500	1,500
Total deposits	24,600		
Est costs	4,500		
Cash in hand	900		
	$30,000		

Borrowed funds

$94,400 @ 17% interest only =	16,728.00

Other expenses

Management fees 8.5%	240.00	
Shire rates	157.00	
Water rates	160.00	
Body corporate	140.00	
Land tax	258.00	
$755.00 x 3	2,265.00	
	18,993.00	

Less income

Rental		
Property (a) 60.00 per week		
(b) 60.00 per week		
(c) 43.00 per week		
$163.00 x 52 =	8,476.00	
	Nett loss (10,517.00) **Tax deductible**	

> 1st year loss reduces your normal taxable income.

Capital Gains @ 15% p.a.– *Based on history of 17% p.a. over 20 years*

Purchase price 123,000

1st year	18,450	4th year	28,061
	141,450		215,135
2nd year	21,223	5th year	32,269
	162,673		246,404
3rd year	24,401	**Capital gain $123,404**	
	187,074		

Our clients range from little investors buying their first properties to large corporations, and we deal with everything from an individual retirement plan to structuring a public company. We have sold in excess of six hundred properties to eastern states clients in the past twenty years, and in all cases our gearing arrangements have been fully accepted by the Taxation Office and our predictions have come through with flying colours.

The following example concerns some clients I met in Sydney twenty years ago.

Eighteen Sales in One Day

They had a taxable income of $100,000 from a pastoral operation, and their accountants wished to reduce it. I arranged the purchase of eighteen 2-bedroom units situated at 305 Harborne Street, Glendalough. (This became my Australian multilisting record of **eighteen sales in one day**.) The purchase price of each was $21,500. They paid 10 per cent deposit on each unit, and their total outlay, including fees, was $48,000. Each of these units is worth $80,000 today, that is $58,500 per unit increase over purchase price in twenty years. In addition, as total rents versus all expenses showed a deficit of $42,000 in the first year (fully tax deductible), their taxable income was reduced to $58,000. The Taxation Office actually contributed half of the deposits by virtue of the deduction. That is, in real terms their return on a $21,500 deposit over twenty years has been $58,500 x 18 or $1,053,000.

Did the same return apply for the people who bought units for cash? If our clients had paid cash, they could have purchased only two units and would have realised capital growth on just two. Today if they sold four of these properties they would own the other fourteen outright. The day will come when, if they sell only one, they will own the other seventeen units. Their loans are all 'interest only'.

The only principal they ever paid was their 10 per cent deposit in the first place. No principal payment will ever be tax deductible. That is why we suggest interest-only loans.

305 Harborne Street, Glendalough.

"Spotters Fees" are OK!

Board staff frequently receive enquires about the legality of "spotters fees".

Section 55(3) of the *Real Estate and Business Agents' Act* states:

An agent or *a developer shall not* whether *directly or indirectly give* any commission, reward or other *valuable consideration to any other person*, not being a licensee who holds a current triennial certificate, *for acting as, or performing any of the functions of a sales representative* unless the other person is a registered sales representative in the service of the agent or developer, as the case may be, in a sales representative. Penalty: $3000.

The important issue is what is involved in "acting as, or <u>performing any of the</u> <u>functions of a sales representative"</u> by a person who is either unlicensed or unregistered.

The Act defines a real estate sales representative as a person who, on behalf of an agent or developer, negotiates a real estate transaction.

If a spotter simply provides information about a possible property transaction by a purchaser/vendor to an agent or sales representative and receives payment for that information, that alone does not constitute performing the functions of a sales representative.

Consequently, if agents and sales representatives offer "spotters fees" for information relating to a real estate transaction, then that payment is allowable under Section 55(3) of the Act.

Spotters Fees Legal

We are happy to talk to clients, accountants and solicitors. This method of tax saving is fully acceptable to the ATO provided income-producing real estate is purchased, rents are declared and the property is held in excess of twelve months. The good news is that accountants are now more willing to recommend real estate as an investment, as they can receive a benefit for doing so. This matter was resolved in 1999, when clarification of the legal situation meant that 'spotter's fees' can be payable. This is also available to you the public.

The Client Who Needs Funds

We do not normally recommend selling. If a client needs funds, my first move is to ask them how much they need. Generally it is not a lot. Then I put it to them that an agent's commission would be say $7,000 to $8,000, whereas they could take equity borrowings out of the property, the interest on which in many cases would be less than the commission. In addition, the loan – even if it were taken out on their own home – would create another tax deduction as long as the money was borrowed for investment purchases. I am also often able to point out that the next year's capital growth would more than cover the interest and the borrowings.

Keeping Them Informed

Another special service we offer to all our property management clients through our Investment Division is to keep them informed regularly on the latest market trends, the value of their properties and future potential rent increases. We send out a newsletter every month and supply monthly as well as annual statements. Their rents are reviewed every six months and their overall situation re-assessed annually. We run weekly investment seminars and encourage them to bring their friends and relatives.

As their property appreciates in value and their equity grows, they can refinance by taking some of the equity out and reinvesting it into additional properties, keeping approximately 20 per cent of the borrowed monies back as a buffer. The buffer, as stated before, is an equity facility (preferably) or a bank account controlled by them for that rainy day.

Looking to the Future

If some of the highest paid people in the world are professional salespeople, where are you? I have mentioned already that top sales representatives earn more than most other professionals – and that 20 per cent of them do 80 per cent of the business. How do you move into that top bracket? The answer, once again, is 'by being different – by being creative'.

The future of residential real estate is in the investment market. All residential real estate offices must get into the investment market – basically because real estate does go up in value in the long term.

Will this happen again? **Of course it will**.

Story of $634,100 sale of a dunny.

States a derelict public lavatory sells for $634,100.

Previously in 1976 a sale fell through for $35,000.

Time Capsule

In each of my seminars I use this as an illustration of taking my audience back in time in a time capsule.

I take them from today back to the last century in an imaginery time capsule.

I have given each of them in theory a copy of the West Australian dated 3 August 1988, hopefully they have all read the paper.

We are now back at the auction in 1976, and I always ask one of them if they would beg, borrow or steal to buy the toilet block knowing what it will be worth in 1988. That person, and every other person in the room unanimously agree they would all buy it!

I questioned that even though it was a public lavatory they would still be prepared to buy it? They all agreed that with that sort of margin they were sure they could pay other people to clean it for them!

I always state that I throw in at least one toilet with every home I have ever sold, sometimes two or three!

THE WEST AUSTRALIAN AUGUST 3 1988

THE WEST AUSTRALIAN WEDNESDAY AUGUST 3 1988

$634,100 — for a dunny

SYDNEY: A derelict Darlinghurst public lavatory sold for a record $634,100 yesterday. A three-storey restaurant is planned for the site.

Sydney City Council town clerk Leon Carter was happy. The last time the council tried to dispose of the 121 square metre site, in 1976, a sale at $35,000 fell through.

The site, between the Darlinghurst fire station and a motel, was valued recently at $180,000.

Reproduced by courtesy of
The West Australian

The Western Mail 1988

MARKET PLACE

A home costs the earth in the world's capitals

Perth is super value

• By GILL WAINWRIGHT

For the price of a one-bedroom flat in Manhattan real estate investors could buy 8.7 houses in Perth. A one-bedroom unit in Manhattan costs a cool $537,500

That's a rather extreme comparison but Perth real estate is still a long way behind other world cities where house prices have gone through the roof.

According to the Real Estate Institute of WA the average. Perth home cost $61,700 in August 1987 — an increase of $6,200 since August 1986.

In New York house prices are increasing by $215 a day and in London by $116.10 a day.

With the average family home costing $215,000 in London, property experts around the world consider Britain's capital something of a bargain basement. San Francisco is far more expensive, though prices are not as high as in New York.

San Francisco agent Rhod Blunt sayshe can find buyers an attractive, two-storey home with three bedrooms in East Bay for about $258,000 — that's only 48km out of town.

"But if you're looking for something downtown, I can get you. a house for $311,750," Mr Blunt said.

"Admittedly, the accommodation will not be big but with two rooms on each floor, it's a good buy.

"It's in the middle of the smog zone, which is why it's a bargain."

Hong Kong has-recently had a property boom which saw apartments soar in price even before they were built.

But land is so scarce there that as-soon as news leaks' out about an impending development potential buyers start queuing outside the builder's offices.

Unable to locate the author of original *Western Mail* article

The article goes on to say you can buy 8.7 homes in Perth instead of a one bedroom apartment in Manhattan New York for $537,500.

Rather than owning the same property outright, with the same money I would leverage myself into perhaps 18 home units in Perth.

If we owned them outright it would be positive gearing, and therefore added to the top of your taxable income and taxed at the maximum rate.

Negative Gearing

In buying the 18 properties through leveraging we would show a loss, therefore reducing your taxable income.

Capital growth

Your capital growth on 18 strata titled home units would be far greater than on 8.7 houses. **WIN WIN WIN!**

Sunday Times July 1, 2001

HAPPY: Mrs Beryl Mason outside the house.

Will this property
go up again?

Reproduced by courtesy
of *The Sunday Times*

$420,000 - and it's the size of a garage

A TINY Sydney house no larger than a standard garage sold for $420,000 in a home buyer's frenzy yesterday.

"I'm very happy," conceded the seller, Mrs Beryl Mason, 80, who bought the bite-size Bronte cottage for $28,000 almost 30 years ago.

"I'm going to be sorry to ieave. I've loved living here — and it's not as small as some people seem to think."

Newcastle builder Goran Ertksson won a bidding war between five home hunters to secure the one-bedroom cottage in Brae St. "It exceeded our expectations," admitted Laing & Simmons listing agent Paul Charles, who said a shortage of housing in the eastern suburbs was driving up real estate values.

The Bronte home, touted as an "old world charmer", is just 4 m wide, with a small bedroom, kitchen, bathroom and lounge room.

The auction attracted more than 150 people.

Who pays for what in the investment property?

Who are your future purchasers? Have a look at your existing rent roll: are any of those clients happy about your services? Are you property managers or rent collectors? Do any of your landlords pay tax? Do any of their friends pay tax? Do any of their children pay tax?

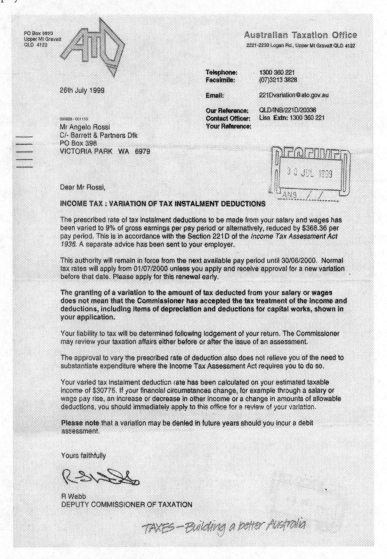

We show our clients how to reduce their tax by buying more properties in April and May and settling them prior to 30 June. We encourage them to pay their interest twelve months in advance, creating large tax rebates. Most of our clients also have a 221D (VTDI Form).

Sale by Auction

I have already mentioned the possibility of selling by auction. This would not be an automatic choice for the ordinary home. Auctions should be considered if there is something special about the property – if it is in some way 'out of the ordinary'. Such was the case with the next example. Another point here is that not every property is a negative gearing prospect.

Auction of 4 Fraser Road, Applecross: The building was an old duplex pair, one sitting on top of the other. The general feeling of the local agents, working on a square metre basis, was that the property ought to bring $2,350,000. I felt we could do better than that if we gave it thorough exposure. We marketed it well throughout the state and to all the foreign embassies in Australia, as well as to major builders and developers and the wealthy generally.

We took the auction to $2,950,000, at which point it was passed in. The couple still left in the bidding couldn't go any higher. We sold it four hours later for $3,060,000.

This was in 2000. The same old duplex pair had last sold in 1968 for $68,000. In 1969 we had had our own wedding reception in the top duplex, so it gave me great pleasure to sell the property for $3,060,000.

AUCTION

4 FRASER ROAD, APPLECROSS

Exquisite River/City Panorama
Absolute Riverfront

- Truly one of the best duplex sites to be offered for sale
- Older type duplex pair
- Existing landsize 1105m²
- Frontage 18.79m²
- Portion of Swan Location 61
- Lot 3; Volume 1065; Folio 657
- Rates: Water $947.20
  Shire $1170.15

Auction: On Site, Saturday 3rd June 2000 at 11.00am On Site

Inspection: Saturdays 12.30pm – 1.30pm

Enquiries: Rory O'Rourke 0418 903 259

O'Rourke
O'Rourke Realty Investments

O'ROURKE SCARBOROUGH
62 Scarborough Beach Rd, Scarborough WA 6019
Fax: (08) 9341 6447
Phone: (08) 9341 6611

If your property and/or business is listed or managed by another agent please disregard this communication

In this next case auctioning was again the best approach, though we had bigger things in mind.

We initially listed two old houses, nos. 170–172 The Esplanade, Scarborough, a prime oceanfront site. There was an uninterrupted view to Rottnest Island, with the ocean panorama stretching from Fremantle to Hillarys, and the zoning – restaurants/shops/offices/residential/accommodation – allowed for interesting possibilities.

I auctioned the two houses on 30 July 1988 for $550,000. Then, on behalf of the same developer, we acquired the two adjoining sites, nos 168 and 174, at $300,000 each. The total land content was thus $1,150,000. The combined property became the site that Sandcastles Holiday Apartments are on today.

We were appointed to sell the end development in conjunction with another agent, and the entire project turned out to be very successful. In fact it is recognised as one of the best developments on the Perth coast, and the units are still very much sought after today. Congratulations must go to the developer, Mr Peter Burns, and the builders, Cooper and Oxley.

The Esplanade, Scarborough Beach, Western Australia.

13

Property Management

Here is a question I asked earlier. I'm repeating it because it's important. Are you a rent collector or a property manager? I am sorry to say it, but most of us are rent collectors.

We can begin to move from being rent collectors to becoming property managers if we take the following proposition seriously. Each of you is more important to your landlords/landladies than are their bankers, solicitors and accountants. How can I possibly say that? Because they have given you the responsibility of managing their biggest asset. Have you taken up the challenge? Or are you doing what run-of the-mill property managers have done for the last thirty years?

Broadly speaking, your landlords will fall into two categories.

- those who let the rent contribute modestly to their income – a modest contribution compared to the size of their investment, however large it is – and rest content in the knowledge that they have solid bricks-and-mortar assets

- those who are chasing capital wealth and tax deductibility

If there are some who fall somewhere in between, they need not concern us here.

If you're the traditional property manager – the one I call a rent collector – you'll handle them in the same way. You'll collect the rent, attend to any repairs, get rid of unsatisfactory tenants and so on. If their accountant persuades them to buy more property, and you're fortunate enough to get the sale and the management, you'll appreciate the extra business.

Note that I've said you'd be fortunate. Why should they give the business to you, considering that you've been doing the bare minimum to look after their interests?

Knowing Your Landlords

Let me take another tack before we pursue this further. How well do you know your landlords?

109

- What is their income?
- Have there been any recent changes in their income/employment situation?
- Do they really need the rental income on top of their normal income?
- Is this additional income putting them in a higher tax bracket?
- What rental income do they receive on any properties other than the ones you manage?
- Do they have a husband/wife?
- How many children do they have and what are their ages?
- What income does each member of the family receive?
- Do they have a tax variation? (See chapter 15.)

Possibly you cannot imagine yourself asking the questions that would bring this information to light. How could a property manager take this line without causing offence? The basic point here is how you see your role. If you begin to take a broad interest in the management of your clients' property investments, you'll present yourself differently. And they will begin to see you differently – as someone who can help them plan their financial future.

Being Proactive

You could certainly take a more creative role in the property management/investment area without necessarily delving as deeply as I'm now inclined to do. One doesn't have to be too bold, for example, to gain some idea of how much equity a client has in a property you're managing for them. And, once you demonstrate the value of your advice, you can move more surely into that wider role.

Your first move into a more proactive role might be a relatively simple one. You could invite a client from the first of the two landlord categories I outlined above, one with substantial equity in their current property holdings, to hear a proposal that would save them tax and increase their wealth. In my experience quite a lot of people find that sort of notion very exciting.

The second of the two categories – 'those who are chasing capital wealth and tax deductibility' – includes a range of clients. They need to be dealt with according to their particular circumstances and attitudes. Some are in a high tax bracket; others are not. Some need little encouragement to buy more property; others are more hesitant. Among this last group are people who are reluctant to take on more debt, even though they are benefiting from negative gearing and their equity position is solid. They represent a lot of potential business, since you have all the facts on your side when you set out to persuade them to take a more forthright approach to property investment.

Of course you have to make sure you do know the facts. As I have said, if you are not prepared to take the step of having an investment coordinator in your office, you need to know all the relevant subjects, which include the Taxation Act (especially Section 221D), the Strata Titles Act, the GST, the capital gains provisions, negative gearing, positive gearing, finance (all the alternatives) and insurance. Most important, you need to keep up with the CCH tax reporting updates.

Information Technology

Most agents see their rent roll as their main asset. In our case it is our whole approach, and especially our philosophy in regard to change, that is the main asset of the business. And more than ever before that involves us in information technology – IT as it is known universally today.

We see

- our seminars
- our website
- our computer programs
- our trained staff

as being worth millions, followed by our large database of clients. While most agents see their rent roll as future sales, we look at our current landlords and tenants and see future purchasers. If the landlord sells, our cash flow drops.

Information technology has changed more in the last decade than in all the time before that. (Can you believe it is only just over ten years ago – on 5 December 1991 to be precise – that the first website was activated?) Are you keeping up with these developments?

Working Smarter

As I say, we see our landlords as future purchasers rather then sellers. Show them you are working smarter, not harder. Set your sights on increasing their capital wealth rather than their taxable income. Every time the sales department lists a property suited for investment, you should scan your landlords to see who is in a position to buy another tax deduction.

We supply monthly statements to our landlords, and along with these we send out newsletters containing helpful information. An annual statement is also supplied at the end of the financial year. (Do you think an annual statement will reduce the accountant's fee? Yes, it should. If it doesn't, ask why.)

In the last chapter I mentioned selling hundreds of Perth properties through one interstate firm of accountants. In fact from 1980 to 1983 I sold as many as 252 Perth properties through them to various people in just one New South Wales country town. As I mentioned, they bought in Perth because they could buy three properties here for every one Sydney. What were they really buying? They were buying tax deductibility and capital wealth. What is the best security in the world to borrow money against? Of course it's real estate, and there is an added bonus there called 'capital growth'.

It is when you are seriously dealing with your clients as investors that you will benefit from knowing as much about them as possible. All those items of information I listed above have a bearing on how you will approach them if you are playing a proactive, creative role in looking after their investment interests.

As an example, consider the situation of a married couple who have decided to buy another property. One decision that has to be made is whether it should be in an individual name or both names. You will be in a better position to advise on this if you know their incomes, their ages, their reasons for investing, what equity they have in each of their properties and their tax situation.

Do I still hear some of you protesting that this is the accountant's role? In my experience they generally record their mistakes six to nine months after the gate closed on 30 June.

The Potential of Your Tenants

A further potential source of business is another group of people whose names appear in your books. I'm referring to your tenants. How many of your former tenants are now among your landlords, thanks to you?

The majority of your renters have the potential to become owner-occupiers. There is then little to stop them moving on to becoming landlords. Many of our previous tenants have gone through this transition. Has it helped the profitability of the firm? It certainly has. How often has it happened to you that a tenant has given notice because an opposition agent has sold them a property, after which you lost all contact with them? Be proactive.

Looking After Your Landlords

Certainly a property manager has more things to consider than selling investment properties. Rents for example. We generally recommend increasing the rent annually as the market warrants. Apart from the state of the market, there is the matter of costs. As rates and taxes, strata levies etc. go up, the property manager must pass the additional cost on to the tenant. Why wait to be told by the landlord? Aren't you the manager? The higher the rent, the more valuable the property is – and that benefits both you and the landlord whose interests you are looking after.

Give your clients broader business advice

Courtesy of CCH

Who are the most important people to the landlord, their bankers, their accountants, their solicitors or their property managers?

Their property managers.

Avoid Tenants from Hell

Another concern of the property manager is landlord protection insurance. We recommend to all our residential landlords that they take out the 'safety net' policy offered by Corporate Home Unit Underwriting. At a cost of $150 per year per property inclusive of GST, tax deductible, who can afford not to have it? Every time I read or see on television a story about 'tenants from hell', I wonder if the managing agent had recommended landlord protection insurance.

Guidance is what people are after. Who knows the most about real estate? The real estate agent. We need to upgrade our services in order to upgrade our image with the public. We need to do more public relations with both landlords and tenants. I repeat: we all need to work smarter rather than harder.

A final thought: All property managers should be property owners. This helps them see things from the landlord's perspective.

landlord's 'safety net' policy

At $150.00 per year who wouldn't have it?

Courtesy of Corporate Home Unit Underwriting

CHU

14

Taxation

What is It?

The Concise Oxford Dictionary states: "tax – contribution levied on persons, property or business for support of Government, as direct, indirect, etc".

How Did It Start?

In the United States of America tax was brought into play to pay for the Civil War and for rebuilding afterwards. How is it still there today?

The Poor

The Government put to the mass population that people earning over a certain figure should pay tax.

Who voted yes? The majority because the majority were poor. The belief was this would bring equality!

Who voted no? The rich. It was they who were being targeted.

Threshold Reduced

Once tax was voted in all the Government had to do was to reduce the threshold. This covered everyone. It is still there today and will always be there in the future.

Australian Tax History

How did tax start here? Did we vote on it? Did we or did our forebears get a say on paying tax? No.

1788

When our first Governor, Governor Phillip arrived in New South Wales in 1788, he had a royal instruction that gave him power to impose taxation if the colony needed it.

The first taxes in Australia were raised to help pay for the completion of Sydney's first jail and provide for the orphans of the colony. Import duties were put on spirits, wine and beer and and later on luxury goods and have spread to every conceivable goods and services since.

What has been your biggest expense throughout your life? While most people asked this question are inclined to mention such things as food, mortgage, education, the answer is in fact tax. And that is only the direct taxes. What about all the indirect taxes? The fact that you never see them being extracted is partly why you get the answer wrong. Yes, the introduction of the GST has made everyone more aware of the indirect element of taxation, but it will not be long before consumers once again pay over their money without a thought that a sizeable portion of it is in fact **tax**. Can that total tax take be reduced? **YES**

The Importance of Privately Owned Real Estate

Privately owned real estate is fast becoming the biggest supplier of residential accommodation. Have you noticed the large number of sales of state housing homes throughout the country? The amount of rent being received on these properties is generally not even covering maintenance.

CCH TAX REFORM

RALPH REVIEW OF BUSINESS TAXATION

Special Tax Week Issue 50   15 November 1999

Introduction	¶890
Alienation of personal services income	¶891
Comprehensive capital allowance system	¶892
Treatment of losses from non-commercial activities	¶893
Improved general anti-avoidance provisions	¶894
Losses on entity interests in loss companies	¶895
Spreading of deductions for tax shelter prepayments	¶896
Dividend streaming and franking credit trading rules	¶897
Rollover provisions for entities	¶898
Involuntary disposal rollovers extended	¶899
Entity taxation related measures	¶900
Allocating income between countries	¶901
Foreign investment in Australia	¶902
Measures affecting offshore investment	¶903
Consultations on other reform issues	¶904

CIRCULATE THIS ISSUE TO:

Special Ralph Review Issue

This Special issue of CCH Tax Week covers the Government's second stage response to the recommendations of the Ralph Review of Business Taxation. It is being distributed free to all subscribers of CCH Tax Week, Australian Federal Tax Reporter, Australian Income Tax Guide, TaxNews, Australian Superannuation Law & Practice, Australian Super News and the Australian Master Tax Guide Updater.

This Special issue is also available on CCH's website at http://www.cch.com.au.

Stage 2 response to Ralph Report

¶890 Introduction

The Treasurer has announced details of Stage 2 of the Government's response to the recommendations contained in the Report of the Ralph Review of Business Taxation — A Tax System Redesigned.

The measures covered in the Treasurer's Press Release No 74 (and Attachments A to O) which are the subject of this Special Issue include: new rules to combat contracting arrangements under which personal services income is alienated through an interposed entity (¶891); the

FOR DISCLAIMER SEE END OF SPECIAL REPORT

¶890

Be informed (by kind permission CCH)

No government in the world can house its people. The Australian Federal Government is no different. Through negative gearing we, the investors, are housing the poor. The Government has nothing to pay out when the private sector is supplying accommodation – no initial capital outlay, no ongoing maintenance.

In 1985 the Labor Government that was then in power played with negative gearing. The headlines read 'Negative Gearing Lost', but this was not actually correct. If you read the fine print you saw that it said negative gearing could be offset against positive. The balance, however, could be carried forward indefinitely – that's deferment, not abolition. Even so it had the effect of drastically reducing private investment in rental property.

In 1988 the Government was alarmed to see what an impact the change was having on the demand for state housing assistance. Very smartly they brought things back to the

way they had been before, and investors could once again claim all losses carried forward in that year and subsequent years. Investment in rental property took off again, relieving the pressure.

So let's be clear. In advocating that estate agents sell the taxation benefits of negative gearing, I am not encouraging them to exploit a loophole. The provision is there because the Federal Government wants it to be there. And politicians of all political persuasions have set us an example: in excess of 60 per cent of Federal Government members have negative-geared real estate. I see this as a clear signal to us, the real estate agents, that we should participate and encourage others to do so.

Capital Gains Tax

But surely capital gains tax has wiped out most of the benefit to the investor? This tax was never the big ogre people were told about. Firstly, we never pay it unless we sell the asset. Secondly, if we do sell, it applies only to the actual gain after taking into consideration all the normal expenses and the inflation component. Thirdly, since the Ralph Report was tabled we pay tax on only 50 per cent of the net gain. Is there any other way we can earn money and pay tax on only half the profit? The notion that whatever profit is generated by real estate will be lost to capital gains tax when the owner eventually sells is a serious misconception.

I am talking of course about the investment property and not the family home, which is exempt. Nor does it generally apply to assets acquired prior to 20/9/1985. Let us look at the practicalities. When we eventually sell, the following occurs:

So, capital gains tax notwithstanding, we should all be chasing capital wealth rather than taxable income. Yet many accountants will tell you that, if through negative gearing you don't pay tax, the problem is deferred and compounded when you eventually sell.

Capital losses may be offset against capital gains realised in a current financial year and can be carried forward indefinitely to be offset against capital gains in subsequent years,ut cannot be offset against other income. Losses are not adjusted for inflation, but are calculated on a normal monetary basis. Death does not constitute a disposal but will give rise to a rollover or a new cost base in the hands of the administrator or the beneficiary, depending on when the asset was acquired – before or after 19 September 1985.

While there is no capital gains tax on a prime residence, if it is vested in a family trust or discretionary trust the tax applies as normal. Capital gains tax does not apply in respect of a forced conversion such as resumption of land (i.e. by government). In regard to real estate investments, the cost of a property includes stamp duty, legal costs and valuation fees as well as advertising and commission on sale.

What are the Accountants and Financial Advisers doing?

YOUR MONEY
THE WEST AUSTRALIAN MARCH 20 2000

Don't leave it all to advisors

If you find yourself defrauded by your lawyer, accountant or financial adviser, join the queue. Vigilance is the best hope of prevention, but clients can also lay a paper trail to justice. DAVID WALKER reports.

When you invested the money, the promised returns of up to 20 per cent seemed wonderful and, although $30,000 was a lot to part with, your family accountants of two decades suggested it and you trusted them without question.

You handed over the money. Three months passed without hearing from the adviser. Six months, still nothing. You started making calls to the accountant that went unreturned.

Finally you went to the firm, only to find the accountant had fled the business, leaving a stunned management initiating investigations on where your money, and that of 20 other clients, had gone.

If this happens to you with your lawyers, accountants or financial advisers, you are not alone.

Studies show that Australia's 1.3 million professionals are

statistically just as likely to commit fraud as other industry groups.

Although it is difficult to pinpoint exactly how much fraud is committed against customers by the professions – partly because only about a third cent of all fraud committed is reported to the police - Det-Chief Insp. Robert Cockerell, of Victoria Police's major fraud group, says 21 per cent of all fraud investigated by his division between 1994 and 1998 was committed by solicitors. A further 19 per cent was by accountants.

Solicitors alone were investigated for the misappropriation of about $64 million,requiring a specially formed squad of 26 investigators, one accountant and a lawyer in the major fraud group.

Cartoon courtesy David Walker/ The Age

If property has been the best performing asset in Britain over 1200 years, and a comparable pattern can be seen in this country's brief history, why haven't most accountants and financial advisers recommended real estate as an investment? One would think that nearly all of them either own or are buying a home, and must have noticed how it had increased in value over the years. Wouldn't it be obvious to recommend investing in real estate?

The answer may lie in the fact that many of them technically don't own a home. They have placed it in their discretionary trust to put it out of the reach of possible creditors. Why haven't they recommended real estate? Because there was nothing in it for them. I need hardly say that in my opinion they have forgone tremendous wealth-creation opportunities by adopting an overcautious risk-avoidance strategy.

Bottom-of-the-Harbour Schemes

Bottom-of-the-harbour schemes, which once were marketed through entrepreneurs and then through financial advisers and accountants, are seen as tax avoidance schemes. The financial advisers and accountants received a commission of somewhere between 3 per cent and 8 per cent of the money collected, which many investors were happy to pay in view of the huge savings they were making on their tax bills. Now those same investors wish they had never heard of the schemes.

There are so many of these schemes that I can't go into particulars. A lot of them are proceeding to the courts as I write, with the tax office challenging their validity. It could be years before they are resolved.

The West Australian Wednesday May 2 2001

Fraud probe over sham tax schemes
By Sue Peacock

UP to 30 tax scheme promoters are under investigation for fraud amid attempts by the Australian Tax Office to stamp out dodgy tax-driven investment schemes via legislation.

The move comes as thousands of West Australians face financial hard-ship after being caught up in question-able tax minimisation investments in the past decade.

Tax Commissioner Michael Carmody told an Australian Institute of Company Directors luncheon in Perth yesterday that

the 1998 introduction of product rulings — designed to protect unwitting investors from being hit with massive tax bills — had failed to stop unscrupulous marketers.

He said in the past week the tax office had written to 300 participants in a scheme marketed over the past three years which sought more than $50 million in deductions.

Investors contributed $10,000, received a $100,000 "loan", resulting in a claimed deduction of $110,000.

"This is clearly a sham, yet people didn't come and ask us for a product ruling or any other approach on the 'too good to be true' tax benefits claimed to be available," he said.

About 30 tax scheme promoters were under investigation.

"We are working with other law enforcement agencies in areas where we believe there may be fraud," he said.

"Proving fraud and getting evidence for fraud is a difficult task, but we will continue to work with other agencies to do that."

You may well ask how such schemes differ from negative gearing investments. Quite simple really: it gets back to the point that without them the Government would be left with a huge problem of housing the poor. Private residential investment gearing, both positive and negative, is supplying 40 per cent of the accommodation for the Australian people, a figure that is growing. The Government forgoes some tax, but it obviously sees this as a lesser burden than having to pay for, manage and maintain public housing.

Who Are the Tax Collectors?

All business proprietors, real estate agents included, have been compelled by the ATO to become tax collectors. All companies, partnerships and trusts are now thoroughly engaged in this role, and it is becoming more onerous each year.

Every business must therefore have a basic knowledge of taxation. We real estate agents collect group tax from employees, payroll tax, GST, BAS statements, wages, commission, superannuation, excesses on superannuation, shire, water, land taxes, etc.

Our attitude has been that, if we have to be so deeply involved in tax, we will really study the subject, and have taken our understanding to the next plateau by keeping abreast of all the tax changes that affect real estate. Our basic tool is a full subscription to CCH. By paying close attention to the tax system and the changes it undergoes, I have been able to ensure that it works for us and for our clients. It can work for each of you also.

The fact that we take a very keen interest in the tax situation of our clients does not mean that we get involved with preparing tax returns. That is a tax agent's or accountant's role. We are showing clients how to reduce their tax in the financial year they are in, not after the gate closes on 30 June. If we do that, we have done our job; then the others can do theirs.

Because we are dealing proactively with our clients on this basis, our investment sales are going through the roof. Your growth potential could easily be tenfold. There is in fact no limit to the extra sales that could be yours if you shift the emphasis of your business to offering clients appropriately tailored negative-gearing options. There is an untapped market out there waiting for you.

It's Time

It's a whole new world of real estate. Are you up to the challenge? Once you have made the effort to understand the tax laws of the land, and implemented the approach I'm recommending, you won't mind collecting tax revenue. The recoupment you receive for your extra sales and new property managements will more than cover the costs of staff collecting tax revenue.

I emphasise again that we recommend to all our clients that they speak to their accountant or financial adviser before committing themselves to anything we might propose.

Reducing Tax

Can you reduce your tax? Hopefully after getting to this stage of my book you will know you can.

You Have a Choice – It's Called Negative Gearing

47% Taxation

Who helps you pay this??

NO ONE!

Mathematically —
If the 47% is not deductible and the 6% is, that's a difference of **53%**

Interest 6%

Who helps you pay this??
Providing the money is borrowed for investment purposes...

1. Tenant
2. Shortfall fully deductible including all other expenses
3. You can get your tax refunded, in fact
4. You don't need to pay it in the first place!

Mathematically, because the 6% interest you pay is tax deductible and the 47% taxation, certainly is not, the gross difference is 53%. Which would you rather pay? I prefer to pay the interest.

15

The Use of Tax Variation

Why do certain fields of employment get set variation? For example, sub-contractors generally pay tax on 20 per cent of their earnings. Farmers can average their income. Well, now we all can vary our tax.

So often your accountant suggests you shouldn't bother – you will get more back at the end of the year. I ask what interest do we get on our money. The answer: Nil. What will be the buying power of that money when we get it back fourteen to eighteen months later? Would the extra take-home pay help to pay your bills today rather than in fourteen months' time?

Read what Angelo and Carmel Rossi have to say. I have now sold them five investment properties to get them to this stage. Are they any better off? Note the size of that tax variation.

Angelo's brother has since bought property, as have his twin sister, nephew, nephew's girlfriend, work mates and friends – all have bought properties from our firm and we manage them all.

The Rossi's Way to Financial Success

O'Rourke
O'Rourke Realty Investments

OUR WAY TO FINANCIAL SUCCESS

I was your average guy, happily married, one child, one dog and a just-paid-off mortgage, working 9 to 5 every day. But I kept asking myself if there was a better way to secure my family's future.

Just listen to our politicians! I realised that when it was time for Carmel (my wife) and me to retire, the age pension would not exist. So I kept searching for an answer – how to become financially secure.

Then one day an ad caught my attention in the local paper – 'Free Wealth Seminar'. Something drew me into reading it, and then to making an appointment to attend the seminar, which was being held in Scarborough that same night. I went along in a very sceptical frame of mind, especially as it was 'free'.

But as I sat there I was amazed at what Rory was saying. Every question was answered right there in front of me, and the answer was: Property!!

I'd always believed investing in property was the key to success, and negative gearing was what this seminar was all about. I came home in a blaze of excitement, and soon my wife was eager to attend the next seminar.

purchased two properties straight away, and my tax rate went from 47 cents in the
to 2% of gross earnings per pay period, i.e. $840 per fortnight to $44 per fortnight.

now progressing well on our financial path, acquiring two further properties and
for our sixth.

'D ONLY KNOWN EARLIER WHAT WE KNOW NOW, WHERE WOULD
BE NOW???

Thanks Rory

A. Rossi

---

12 September 1999

To: Rory O'rourke

RE: A BIG THANKYOU

Rory

Your FREE Wealth Creation Seminar was the BEST.

The information and knowledge that we have Gained will NO DOUBT help us to secure our financial future safely and successfully. A full credit to you and your Professional staff.

If only we had known about your seminar years ago.

Where would we be today????

Kindest Regards

Angelo & Carmel Rossi

Angelo
15 Pas
Beaconsfield WA 6162

We purchased two properties straight away, and my tax rate went from 47 cents in the dollar to 2% of gross earnings per pay period, i.e. $840 per fortnight to $44 per fortnight.

We are now progressing well on our financial path, acquiring two further properties and looking for our sixth.

IF WE'D ONLY KNOWN EARLIER WHAT WE KNOW NOW, WHERE WOULD WE BE NOW???

2221-2233 Logan Rd., Upper Mt Gravatt QLD 4122
PO Box 9990 Upper Mt Gravatt QLD 4122

Telephone: 1300 360 221
Facsimile: (07)3213 3828

Our Reference: INB/221D/QLD/25759
Contact Officer: Variations Officer 27 **Extn:** 1300 360 221
Your Reference:

5 January 1999

RECEIVED
0 8 JAN 1999
ANS / /

Mr Angelo Rossi
GPO Box 398
VICTORIA PARK WA 6979

Dear Mr Rossi

INCOME TAX : VARIATION OF TAX INSTALMENT DEDUCTIONS

The prescribed rate of tax instalment deductions to be made from your salary and wages has been varied to 2% of gross earnings per pay period. This is in accordance with the Section 221D of the *Income Tax Assessment Act 1936*. A separate advice has been sent to your employer.

This authority will remain in force from the next available pay period until **30 June 1999.** Normal tax rates will apply from 1 July 1999 unless you apply and receive approval for a new variation before that date. Please apply for this renewal early.

The granting of a variation to the amount of tax deducted from your salary or wages does not mean that the Commissioner has accepted the tax treatment of the income and deductions shown in your application.

Your liability to tax will be determined following lodgement of your return. The Commissioner may review your taxation affairs either before or after the issue of an assessment.

The approval to vary the prescribed rate of deduction also does not relieve you of the need to substantiate expenditure where the Income Tax Assessment Act requires you to do so.

Your varied tax instalment deduction rate has been calculated on your estimated taxable income of $43,697.00. If your financial circumstances change, for example through a salary or wage pay rise, an increase or decrease in other income or a change in amounts of allowable deductions, you should immediately apply to this office for a review of your variation.

Please note that a variation may be denied in future years should you incur a debit assessment.

Yours faithfully

R Webb
DEPUTY COMMISSIONER OF TAXATION

TAXES—Building a better Australia

125

PO Box 9990
Upper Mt Gravatt
QLD 4122

Australian Taxation Office
2221-2223 Logan Rd., Upper Mt Gravatt QLD 4122

3rd August 2000

8 AUG 2000
ANS / /

Telephone:	1300 360 221
Facsimile:	(07)3213 3188
Email:	ITWvariation@ato.gov.au
Our Reference:	QLD/INB/ITWV/46049
Contact Officer:	Anne Extn: 1300 360 221
Your Reference:	

002080 - 000992
Mr Angelo Rossi
C/- Barrett & Partners Dfk
PO Box 398
VICTORIA PARK   WA   6979

Dear Mr Rossi,

VARIATION OF INCOME TAX WITHHOLDING RATE

The prescribed income tax withholding rate to be applied to the witholding payments listed below has been varied to 1% per payment period. This is in accordance with section 15-15 of Schedule 1 of the *Tax Administration Act 1953*. Concessional rebates have been considered when calculating this rate.

A separate notice stating this has been sent to your payer.

WITHHOLDING PAYMENTS:
   Salary & Wages

This arrangement will remain in force from the next available payment period until 30/06/2001. Normal income tax withholding rates will apply from 01/07/2001 unless you apply and receive approval for a new variation before that date. Please apply for this renewal early.

The granting of a variation to your income tax withholding rate does not mean that the Commissioner has accepted the tax treatment of the income and deductions shown in your application.

Your liability to tax will be determined following lodgment of your income tax return. The Commissioner may review your taxation affairs either before or after the issue of an assessment.

Your varied income tax withholding rate has been calculated on your estimated taxable income of $24,013. If your financial circumstances change, for example due to an increase in income or a decrease in amounts of allowable deductions, you should immediately apply to this office for a review of your variation.

TAXES—Building a better Australia

WELCOME TO 45 LANGLEY CRESCENT INNALOO

VILLA – $249,950

TOWNHOUSE – $299,950

FEATURES INCLUDE:
- ◆ 3 SPACIOUS BEDROOMS
- ◆ LUXURIOUS BATHROOMS
- ◆ QUALITY DALE ALCOCK CONSTRUCTION
- ◆ PRIME PARK LOCATION
- ◆ PRIVATE COURTYARD
- ◆ LARGE TILLED LIVING AREAS

Rory O'Rourke

0418 903 259 or 9341 6611

www.orourke.com.au

This is Angelo Rossi's latest property – With this his tax should be down to 0% and he will start building tax credits.

16

GST and Real Estate

The introduction of the Goods and Services Tax is a sound economic decision by John Howard. You might not like it, but after all it's only a replacement for wholesale tax. We all need to forget the word GST and get on with life. From the large corporations right through to you and me, all now pay GST. If you don't want to pay GST, don't buy the item.

The Goods and Services Tax is now a part of the new tax system. GST is a broad-based multi-staged tax on the supply of – yes – goods and services, which is designed to be revenue neutral for registered businesses. Who pays it? The ultimate consumer. Who is responsible for the payment being made to the Australian Taxation Office? The supplier, not the buyer.

How does GST work? Outputs and outputs tax, inputs and input tax credits. Then setting off input tax credits against output tax. The GST rate is 10 per cent. This could be increased with the approval of the state and territory governments.

Implications of the GST for Real Estate and Business Agents

When a business is sold as a going concern, whether or not the sale includes commercial property, the total sale may be treated as a GST-free supply. That is, no GST is payable on the sale. Qualifications must be met.

No GST is payable on the sale of an established normal residence, but it does apply to the agent's commission.

There is no GST payable on residential rents. GST does, however, apply to an agent's management fees on rent collection. For example:

Rental of $200 per week = $10,400 per annum

Management fee 7% = $728 per annum

The GST is 10% of the management fee = $72 per annum

Commercial Properties

The agent principal (usually a landlord) makes the supply of a commercial property to a tenant. The landlord or the agent can issue it. It needs to be defined as to who is going to issue the tax invoice in each case.

All sales of commercial property, i.e. non-residential property, are subject to GST if the vendor is registered or should be registered at the point of settlement.

When leasing commercial property, the registered lessors are liable for GST in regard to new leases entered into.

Various transitional provisions and liability for GST under leases apply. Whether a landlord has liability will depend on numerous situations such as:

- when the lease commenced
- when the lease finishes
- when there is a rent review
- the basis of the rent review
- the GST status of the tenant

It is vital that the landlord knows the GST status of the tenant.

New Homes

New homes (never been lived in) or ones under construction attract GST. GST is payable on the sale of a new residential premises whether bought by an owner-occupier or an investor.

Subdivided Residential Land

Sales of residential land by a developer are subject to GST. Private sales made by a private vendor, i.e. not a registered business, are not subject to GST.

17

The Advantages of Negative Gearing Over Positive Gearing

Most accountants will tell you negative gearing is about losing money and positive gearing is about making money. Generally they have missed the point. They are talking cash flow negative or cash flow positive. This is not the only consideration. There are many deductions, such as depreciation on buildings and chattels, borrowing costs and prepayment of interest.

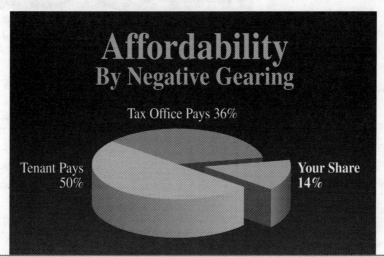

Affordability
By Negative Gearing

Tax Office Pays 36%

Tenant Pays 50%

Your Share 14%

This example is showing you during the entire life of the investment, your input is only 14% of the total cost.
Could this be reduced to nil? Definitely, subject to further attention to tax planning.

Recommending negative gearing is just too much trouble for many accountants. For one thing, they would have to keep up with all the tax changes, which are considerable. And it's a much more comfortable life if they don't have to concern themselves with such things as suggesting prepayment of interest and applying for a tax variation. Better to wait until after 30 June when it's all too late.

Negative gearing is one of the best forms of tax deductibility a person can get today. There is no limit of claim. Whether $1500 or $150,000 is being sought as a tax deduction, it can be created through the purchase of investment real estate.

A person's home is worth $160,000 and has a clear title; he can borrow $128,000 against it (80 per cent of value) through an equity loan.

With this money, he could buy three properties worth $100,000 each or, alternatively, he could buy two properties and prepay interest of say $30,000.

If his income was $80,000 and he settled these properties on 29 June, this would reduce his taxable income to $50,000 and save him $14,000 to $15,000 in tax.

A person's home is worth $160,000 and has a clear title; she can borrow $128,000 but she only borrows $40,000 against it.

With this she purchases an additional property worth $100,000. The deposit is $25,000, establishment costs are $5,000, the new mortgage is $75,000 and she leaves a buffer of $10,000 in an equity facility. Voluntary savings might be set at $5,000 per annum.

The day settlement takes place the client applies for a tax variation. This dramatically affects their cash flow. Instead of waiting for a tax rebate in fourteen to eighteen months' time, they don't pay that proportion of tax in the first place. This helps pay the bills.

Page one of the application for your tax variation

Managing the Investment

As I have mentioned already, we always recommend that an equity facility account be established to accommodate the entire investment proposal, and generally suggest investors start it with some of their own cash funds if they have it. This money is there to give them peace of mind. It is recommended they have all their rental income paid into this account along with their cash savings (set figure agreed to, in the example above $5,000 per annum) and their tax savings (this being the extra money they are taking home through the negative gearing tax saving). All the expenses are paid out of this account including the interest on the equity borrowings and the shortfalls.

By doing this we have created double entry bookkeeping. Whether the investor has one investment property or ten, the same account can be used. As long as these funds are used for investment purchases, they are tax deductible.

Why isn't everybody doing it? We have numerous clients who have reduced their tax substantially through negative gearing. Some still pay some tax; some pay no tax at all. Some get Austudy for their children. Some have tax credits carried forward such that they might never pay tax again. (Tax credit surpluses can be carried forward indefinitely.)

How the Rules Have Changed

I have mentioned already changes to the rules to do with negative gearing that took place on 17 July 1985 and again on 15 September 1987. On that second date the Federal Treasurer announced that the original rules that had applied before 17 July 1985 would be reintroduced, i.e. the full interest costs of owning and maintaining rental properties would be again tax deductible against income from any source.

As a result of this all expenses, including interest payments on rental property loans (including 'quarantined' interest carried forward from 17 July 1985 to 15 September 1987), are fully deductible against income from all other sources irrespective of when the property was acquired.

As far as building depreciation goes, 4 per cent depreciation on new buildings built between 17 July 1985 and 15 September 1987 would be good for twenty-five years. New buildings erected since 15 September 1987 would be allowed depreciation of 2.5 per cent and this would be good for forty years. The depreciation allowance on new income-producing buildings was reduced except where:

- construction was pursuant to a contract entered into on or before that date, or
- the land was acquired on or before 15 September 1987 and the borrowings used to finance the construction were contracted for the purpose on or before that date

Rental properties previously entitled to the 4 per cent, or now 2.5 per cent, depreciation allowance will continue to be eligible for the deduction at that rate.

Tax Deductible Items Against Rental Income

The following list constitutes a comprehensive guide as to what can be claimed in your income tax return against your rental income.

1. **Advertising:** All advertising costs associated with obtaining a tenant for the property are allowable

2. **Agents fees and commission:** All fees (e.g. Inspection, leasing etc.) and monthly commission charges are fully deductible.

3. **Borrowing expenses:** The costs of procuring a mortgage (i.e. valuation costs, loan establishment fees etc) are deductible over 5 years where the loan is for 5 years or more. If the loan is for a period less than 5 years the costs are deductible over the period of the loan.

4. **Cleaning:** The cost of cleaning a rental property between tenants is deductible. This even includes the cost of detergents etc.

5. **Depreciation:** It is permissible to claim depreciation on furniture, fixtures, window treatments, floor coverings and other items such as stoves, hot water systems, bores etc. The rates of depreciation vary from 7½ to 30% depending on the item. To ascertain the correct rate a current year booklet should be utilized.

6. **Depreciation allowance of new property:** 2½% of the building content of the property is allowable for the term that the property is held as an investment. If the property is sold to another investor the deductibility flows on to the new owner.

7. **Electricity:** Costs to the landlord between tenants are deductible.

8. **Inspection visits:** A landlord may claim the cost of travelling to his rental property if the specific purpose of the trip is to inspect the property or carry out or organize repairs. Please note landlords in the country can claim the cost of a trip to Perth including accommodation, **BUT NOT** if the main purpose of the trip is for a holiday.

9. **Insurance:** deductions are allowable for premiums paid in respect of household contents and mortgage insurance policies

10. **Landlord's protection insurance:** The premium is tax deductible on this cover, which is highly recommended to all Landlord's

11. **Interest on loans:** Interest on loans procured to either assist in the acquisition of a rental property, additions to the property or to carry out major renovations are all deductible against rental income

12. **Prepayment of interest in advance:** You can prepay interest up to 13 months in advance. i.e. If you bought a property and settled it on June 29th, by prepaying 12 months interest in advance you have 1 days rent, and 366 days interest expense, thus dramatically reducing this years tax.

13. **Lawnmowing and garden maintenance:** All expenses associated with these items including tree lopping are allowable.

14. **Management levies:** Strata levies for home units, villas etc are deductible except for levies utilized to carry out capital improvements, alterations or additions.

15. **Pest control:** Costs of this nature are also deductible

16. **Purchase costs:** These costs (e.g. Stamp Duty on transfer, Settlement agents fees etc.) are added on to the purchase price of the property and claimable in full when the property is sold.

17. **Rates:** Council and water rates together with land tax are allowable in full.

18. **Sundry:** There may be other isolated items that could be deductible. A qualified Accountants advice should be sought for these items.

19. **Telephone, stationery and postage:** These costs, if directly related to the property are deductible.

20. **Accountant's fees:** Fees for advice or tax preparation.

21. **Bank fees and charges:** Fees and charges directly related to the income and expenses of the investment property

22. **Legal costs:** For rent recovery and/or eviction charges

Summary

Always look at your tax in April of the year we are in, once 30th June has gone it is too late. Look at what you earned at from 1st April of the previous year to 31st March of the current year, and you should have a good idea of what you will make.

Tax Planning

Tax planning is the process of organizing your affairs so that as far as legally or commercially possible, the liability of your tax commitment is minimized.

Negative Gearing

Negative gearing is the best form of positive gearing.

Negative Gearing with property is probably one of the most proven and safe methods of reducing your tax.

Accountant

Always consult your accountant or financial planner prior to committing yourself.

18

Inflation

How does inflation work?

Inflation is the biggest 'bank robber' of all time. It takes wealth from the wealthy who hold paper script. Inflation is often controlled by governments; you could say it is a form of taxation.

When making investment decisions with inflation in mind, it is important to get away from thinking exclusively of income. Income can rarely compensate for the destructive effect of inflation. One must invest in commodities that offer not only a return but also capital growth.

Inflation influences all market cycles from the boom and bust of business to commodity market price fluctuations.

How Inflation Erodes Savings

There is a common misunderstanding that if you are receiving 5 per cent interest, and inflation is running at 5 per cent, you are breaking even. This is not so:

If you invest	$10,000
Interest at 5%	500
Total	$10,500
Less income tax (35%)	175
Balance	$10,325

Your bank balance reads $10,325 at the end of the first year, but how about the inflation? Let's have a look at the complete picture:

Investment	$10,000
Interest at 5%	500
Bank balance after 1 year	$10,500
Less income tax on interest	175
	$10,325
Less inflation at 5%	516
Balance	$ 9,809

That is $191 less than you had a year earlier. If you depend on the interest to live on, the future is a lot worse – you are going backwards. Inflation is eating away at the true value of your money.

When inflation is running high and interest is also high, the problem is compounded. I have seen people's lump-sum superannuation diminish to one-third in buying power over a ten-year period when both inflation and interest ran at 10 per cent.

The Solution

Without doubt, those who triumph over inflation are the people who leverage themselves into real estate and take advantage of economic cycles. Real estate can be geared negatively or positively, and it can deliver healthy capital growth over a five to seven-year period.

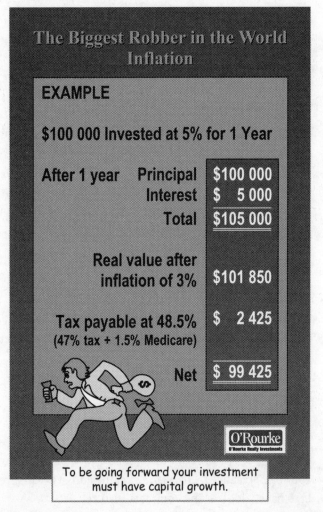

**The Biggest Robber in the World
Inflation**

EXAMPLE

$100 000 Invested at 5% for 1 Year

After 1 year	Principal	$100 000
	Interest	$ 5 000
	Total	$105 000
	Real value after inflation of 3%	$101 850
	Tax payable at 48.5% (47% tax + 1.5% Medicare)	$ 2 425
	Net	$ 99 425

O'Rourke
O'Rourke Realty Investments

To be going forward your investment must have capital growth.

19

Becoming a Property Developer

How can one get started in property development? Most of us have flair and most of us will get a thrill out of creating something. Your own home can be your first project – and so often it is, accidentally or otherwise.

If you buy a second home that needs restoration and sell your own prime residence, there will be no capital gains tax to pay. Suppose you work on your new property and sell it in say eighteen months' time – still you have no capital gains tax to pay, because you have sold your own prime residence again. If you did most of that work yourself, your capital gain will be so much the bigger.

This can grow to where you might move on to duplexes. You can buy a home on a duplex block and, while you are renovating the existing house, a builder can be constructing your new home in the backyard. Sell your home, move into the new one and on you go again. We renovated fourteen homes while our children were young, living in four of them while we were renovating. It was difficult but worthwhile.

Small Development Examples

In the mid-1980s we bought a single residential house on a single residential block at 1 Hugh Street, Waterman. This was a huge, long home with verandahs. On looking at tax maps and over the back fence, we became aware of a large vacant portion of land. We approached the neighbour at the rear, suggesting that he might like to install a swimming pool or perhaps reduce his mortgage. He was all ears. Buying 300 m² of his land and amalgamating it with our block of approximately 700 m² would give us a duplex site. Negotiations took place and we paid the couple $4,500.

PARCEL OF LAND PORTION OF SWAN LOCATION 548
AND BEING LOT 5 ON DIAGRAM 52892
CERTIFICATE OF TITLE : VOLUME 1478 FOLIO 999
LOCAL AUTHORITY CITY OF STIRLING
LOCALITY WATERMAN INDEX PLAN PERTH 2000 07 36
NAME OF BUILDING ERIN'S HIDAWAY
ADDRESS FOR SERVING OF 5 HUGH ST WATERMAN
NOTICES ON COMPANY 6020

STRATA PLAN 6082

OFFICE USE ONLY

LODGED 11 5 18

EXAMINED 17 5 18 18

REGISTERED

OFFICE OF TITLES

REGISTRAR OF TITLES

A PHOTO COPY
RAM No
PLAN
ON

Pt 203   Pt 204   Pt 205

TO PATIO 1-34

STREET

HUGH

5

4

The land in question

300 m²   208

211

STEFFANONI, EWING & CRUICKSHANK
LICENSED SURVEYORS & CIVIL ENGINEERS
282 ROKEBY ROAD, SUBIACO 6008

SCALE LINKS TO AN INCH 1:500

SCHEDULE OF UNIT ENTITLEMENT		OFFICE USE ONLY CURRENT Cs. of TITLE	
LOT No.	UNIT ENTITLEMENT	VOL.	FOL.
1	1		
2	1		
AGGREGATE	2		

SURVEYOR'S CERTIFICATE

I hereby certify that the building shown on the plan is within the external surface boundaries of the parcel and where eaves or guttering project beyond those boundaries, that a registered easement has been granted as an appurtenance of the parcel or, where the projection is over a road that the Local Authority has consented thereto.

DATE 8 March 1978 LICENSED SURVEYOR.

APPROVED BY THE TOWN PLANNING BOARD
FOR THE PURPOSES OF THE STRATA TITLES ACT 39 OF 1966

DATE 9 MAY 1978 CHAIRMAN.

63770/9/70-2M-0/MGD

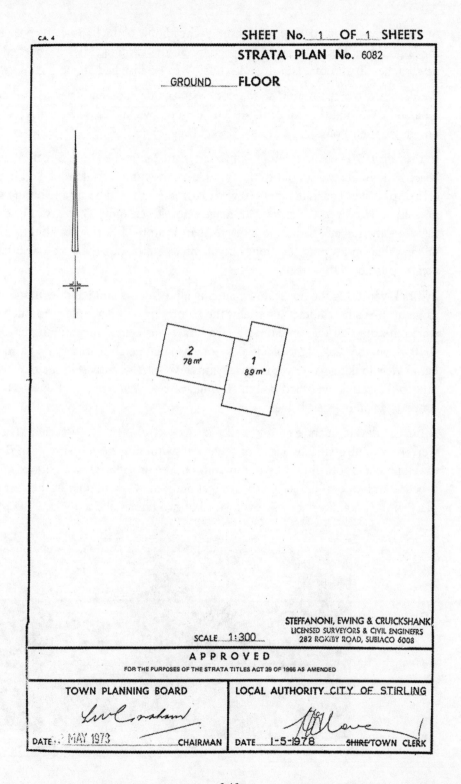

C.A. 4

STRATA PLAN No. 6082

GROUND FLOOR

2
78 m²

1
89 m²

STEFFANONI, EWING & CRUICKSHANK
LICENSED SURVEYORS & CIVIL ENGINEERS
282 ROKEBY ROAD, SUBIACO 6008

SCALE 1:300

APPROVED

FOR THE PURPOSES OF THE STRATA TITLES ACT 39 OF 1966 AS AMENDED

TOWN PLANNING BOARD

DATE 2 MAY 1973   CHAIRMAN

LOCAL AUTHORITY CITY OF STIRLING

DATE 1-5-1978   SHIRE/TOWN CLERK

At this point we put a parapet wall through the middle of the house and enclosed the large verandahs, thus creating space for all the extra facilities we needed – new kitchen, bathroom, laundry and toilet. We also installed an extra carport.

We designed the renovation so we could strata title each and then sold them separately. We sold the front property to a couple we knew, as we had recently purchased their home at 13 Muller Street, Trigg.

In the late 1970s we had bought a property situated at 21 James Street, North Beach. The home was an old-timer, weatherboard with a Bristile roof, and it sat on a duplex site. The initial thought was to demolish the old home and build two new units. However, the current frontage setback was only 13 feet, whereas at that time the setback had to be 25 feet. Apart from the fact that we could put a dollar value on keeping the front alignment where it was, the house also had great views down the street.

By brick-veneering the house and changing all the doors and window frames, it came up like a new home. Internally, the bathroom, laundry, toilet and kitchen were renovated. At the same time, a new house was being built running north–south down the back of the block, positioned so that nearly all rooms had a good ocean view looking west over the backyards. We subsequently sold the new rear unit to the couple who had bought 1 Hugh Street, Waterman, and onsold that property again on their behalf.

A further development example is 25–27 Corbett Street, Scarborough. There were two homes side by side, one with a swimming pool at the rear. The development is now three 3-bedroom units on 25 Corbett Street with the existing 3-bedroom home still at 27 Corbett Street and a new townhouse at the rear in place of the pool. Five homes now instead of two homes and a pool.

25-27 Corbett Street, Scarborough

25-27 Corbett Street, Scarborough

Yet another example is 27–29 Albemarle Street, Scarborough. The couple that owned number 27 wanted a new 3-bedroom unit in lieu of their older home. By giving up their title (in a legally bound contract, naturally) they were able to choose their position on the site, the layout they wanted etc.

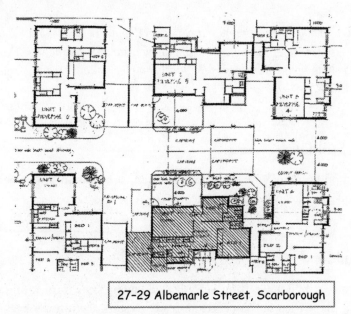

27-29 Albemarle Street, Scarborough

We arranged for the developer to pay for their rental costs while construction was taking place, plus storage costs for their furniture, cost of transport, cost of telephone transfer, cost of stamp duty on the purchase of the new unit and payment of the commission on the sale of the old house and purchase of their new residence.

Property Developments – Building New Dwellings

The secrets of being a successful property developer are:

1. Own the land outright (if possible)

   If you can own the land outright, should there be a downturn you will be able to carry yourself through.

2. Pay interest in advance

   Try to be in a position to prepay your interest, allowing 3–4 months' buffer from completion date.

3. Remember you have partners

   Who are they?

   - The builder, who needs a profit
   - The bank, which wants interest
   - Marketing fees

The first two are self-explanatory. Why marketing fees?

Who stands to make the most profit out of the development? You do. You do not make a profit until the last unit is sold, so make sure you allow a sum for marketing. The interest you are paying is likely to be far in excess of the marketing fee. It could mean a sale within 30 days instead of 120 days.

Owner-Builder

If you plan on building your own home, you must be careful. In some states the rules are that you must keep it for seven years.

Spec Builder

If you are a spec builder starting out, plan on having say a duplex under construction, another on the market and a third site ready to start. Continuity enables you to keep your tradespeople in regular work. Loss of good tradespeople can be a serious setback.

Too often the builder starting out wants to see the profit from the first development prior to starting the second. Because wages still have to be paid in the down time or lost time, they could well go broke. The one-off development generally cannot carry that.

Scheduling

Time management in scheduling is of utmost importance to the flow of each job and the continuity of work, with your tradespeople going from one job to the next.

Another very important factor is quantity estimating. Even if you can do your own, get it double-checked. Each of your developments is different and the costings to go with it are different also. One major omission can mean it is your last development.

Make sure you are not undercapitalised. If it means bringing in partners, do so. **No-one ever went broke making a profit**. Thirty-three and a half per cent of something is better than one hundred per cent of nothing.

20

Successful Project Marketing

Marketing is what it is all about – today and in the future. Marketing is more important in real estate than in any other selling field. Too many representatives are said to be either a good 'listing' representative or a good 'selling' representative. This is not good enough. You need to be the best marketer of both listing and selling.

What is marketing? Is it advertising in the press, radio and TV, producing pamphlets and so on? Or is there more?

Listings don't always have to be worked for, however, as the following story relates. One day my son Jarrad took a telephone call. The caller had commercial properties that were proving difficult to move, though they had been on the market for some time through normal commercial and industrial agents. Jarrad suggested that our firm could sell their properties through our weekly investment seminars. That inquiry resulted in us listing sixteen commercial units. Of course we would never have received that call had we not established some reputation for selling commercial property.

Commercial properties can certainly be professionally marketed to the wider community. Most small investors will buy residential because that's what they understand; with your guidance they could become interested in a spread of investments.

Project Marketing

Let us look at some successful marketing projects we have carried out.

30 Erindale Road, Balcatta (The project that Jarrad took the call on)

- Name changed from Erindale Home Base to Balcatta Commercial Centre.
- Complex strata-titled to sixteen individual units, each with its own volume and folio numbers under the Strata Titles Act.
- Fifteen of the units sold on the basis of a commercial return of 8.75 per cent. (The remaining unit was vacant, has since sold.)
- Ninety per cent of the properties sold to investors who attended our investment seminars. (My own family purchased two of them.)

- Assessments carried out on each unit with the aid of computer programs.
- Strata management and most of the property management taken on by our firm.
- Most units sold with no deposit outlay on the part of the investor client.

"Erindale Commercial Centre"

CAN POSITIVE GEARED COMMERCIAL PROPERTY BE NEGATIVELY GEARED
FOR INVESTMENT PURPOSES.

ERINDALE COMMERCIAL CENTRE
30 ERINDALE ROAD, BALCATTA

EXAMPLE ONE: NIL DEPOSIT

	1 UNIT	2 UNITS	3 UNITS
PURCHASE PRICE (@300,000 PER UNIT	300,000	600,000	900,000
FIRST MORTGAGE (INCLUDING COLLATERAL SECURITY)	320,000	640,000	960,000
CASH REQUIRED NIL PROVIDING SUFFICIENT EQUITY IN OTHER PROPERTIES			
1 UNIT			
FIRST MORTGAGE 320,000 @ 7.5% Int only	24,000		
(BORROWED EXTRA 20,000 TO COVER ESTABLISHMENT COSTS)			
2 UNITS			
FIRST MORTGAGE 640,000 @ 7.5% Int only		48,000	
(BORROWED EXTRA 40,000 TO COVER ESTABLISHMENT COSTS)			
3 UNITS			
FIRST MORTGAGE 960,000 @ 7.5% Int only			72,000
(BORROWED EXTRA 60,000 TO COVER ESTABLISHMENT COSTS)			
LESS RENTAL INCOME PA 8.75% NET ON PURCHASE PRICE	26,250	52,500	78,750
SHORTFALL PER ANNUM/POSITIVE	2,250	4,500	6,750
LESS EXPENSES: NIL (PAID BY TENANT)			
AN INDIVIDUAL (HIGH TAX PAYER) SHOULD PRE-PAY INTEREST 12 MONTHS IN ADVANCE TO OBTAIN THE COMMERCIAL CONSIDERATION	23,680	47,360	71,040
NET SHORTFALL PRIOR TO OTHER TAX DEDUCTIONS	21,430	42,860	64,290

PRE-PAY INTEREST
AN INDIVIDUAL CAN PRE-PAY UP TO 13 MONTHS INTEREST IN ADVANCE.
COULD YOU USE A DEDUCTION OF $21,430 THIS YEAR?
NATURALLY YOUR CAPITAL GROWTH IS NOW ON AN EXTRA   300,000   600,000   900,000

"Erindale Commercial Centre"

COMMERCIAL PROPERTIES GROUP

Level 1, 20 Kings Park Road, West Perth, Western Australia 6005, Australia
PO Box 900, West Perth, Western Australia 6872, Australia
Telephone +618 9322 7755   Facsimile +618 9322 6020

8 January 2002

Mr Rory O'Rourke
O'Rourke Realty Investments
62 Scarborough Beach Road
SCARBOROUGH WA 6019

Dear Rory

**Re: SALE OF ERINDALE COMMERCIAL CENTRE
        30 ERINDALE ROAD BALCATTA**

We wish to acknowledge your application and dedication in marketing and selling the
units in the above centre.

Optimum selling prices were asked at the outset and we were delighted that all of the
units were sold on these most competitive market capitalisation rates.

During the term of your agency we experienced an unprecedented standard of
professionalism from both yourself and your staff. In all cases settlements were
effected on time due to your ability to communicate with and assist purchasers with
their financial dealings with lenders and guidance with completion of documentation.

Once again we appreciate your sterling efforts in achieving these sales on our behalf
and we look forward to maintaining our association with you.

Yours faithfully
Commercial Properties Pty Ltd
ABN 76 008 987 942

Clive Hartz

Fifteen Sold in One Day

Barnes Road, Innaloo

- Block of ten 3-bedroom, 2-bathroom villas in a security complex.
- Marketed through our investment seminars.
- All sold to one client.
- Cash deposit – nil.
- Same client bought five other properties on the same day.
- Fifteen new property managements and a new strata management for our firm.

Ad for the first week

INNALOO   **FROM $139,750**

CORNER MORRIS ROAD & BARNES ROAD

Price Range from **$139,750** _to_ **$146,950**

Congratulations to Tarca Homes for developing this magnificent Tuscan Development.

It's a pleasure to offer these 3 bed/2 bath luxury villas, each with a family room, gourmet kitchen, electronic security to external garage and internal enclosure. The nicest development in Innaloo!

For further details phone **Yano Palazzo 0412 934 247** or **Rory O'Rourke 0418 903 259**.

We have a large range of units throughout the metropolitan area to view. _Areas include: Como, South Perth, Jolimont, Balcatta, Innaloo, Doubleview & Scarborough._

SPEAK TO THE LEADERS IN UNIT MARKETING

RORY O'ROURKE
PRINCIPAL

O'Rourke

O'ROURKE REALTY INVESTMENTS
62 Scarborough Beach Road, Scarborough, 6019
9341 6611 Facsimile: 9341 6447

TARCA HOMES
BUILDERS & DESIGNERS
PETER OR PHIL TARCA
76 Fairfield St., Mt. Hawthorn 6016
9444 2312

INVESTMENT PROPOSAL REDUCING YOUR TAX AND PROVISIONAL TAX (IF APPLICABLE)

Purchase Innaloo development. Situated on the corner of Barnes Road and Morris Road, Innaloo. Buy all 10 units.

Asking price on:	Unit 1	$144,950	Unit 6	$143,950
	Unit 2	$139,750	Unit 7	$145,950
	Unit 3	$143,950	Unit 8	$145,950
	Unit 4	$143,750	Unit 9	$146,750
	Unit 5	$142,950	Unit 10	$146,950
				$1,444,900

Suggest an offer of	$1,420,000	
Costs:		
Stamp Duty	55,425	
Transfer Fees	930	
Settlement Costs	4,000	
TOTAL COST	$1,480,355	
Borrow say $1,100,000 @ 8%		$88,000

RENTAL INCOME

$170 x 50 x 10	$85,000	
Less 25% (outgoing)		
Shire, water insurance,		
Strata, management fee	$21,250	$63,750
SHORTFALL		$24,250
Shortfall carried forward		$24,250

OTHER TAX DEDUCTIONS (PER YEAR)

20% of Borrowing costs, of say $5,000	1,000
Depreciation of chattels 3,000 x 14% x 10	4,200
Depreciation on building $80,000 x 2.5% x 10 units	20,000
TOTAL TAX DEDUCTION	**$49,440**

Say at 48.5 cents in the dollar what you saved in tax pays the shortfall.
Estimated capital growth on this purchase alone in Innaloo based on the last ten years at 0.2% p.a.

The following calculations are at 10% capital gain p.a.

PURCHASE PRICE		$1,420,000		
	1st year	$ 142,000	4th Year	$ 189,002
		$1,562,000		$2,079,022
	2nd year	$ 156,200	5th Year	$ 207,902
		$1,718,200		**$2,286,922**
	3rd Year	$ 171,820		
		$1,890,020		

That is an increase of $866,922 in five years.
Based on total input of $380,355 – say, $380,000

That is a return of 228%, or 45.62% p.a.

Ad for week two

All ten sold to one investor, plus four other properties on the same day.

24 Onslow Street, South Perth

- Four-storey security complex comprising seventeen units – sixteen 1-bedroom and one 2-bedroom.
- All marketed on the basis of tax minimisation and capital growth.
- Great location – opposite Perth Zoo administrative quarters.
- Building interior gutted and totally refurbished throughout with quality fittings.
- Strata-titled to create seventeen individual titles.
- Four units sold to one client, two each to several more.
- Biggest selling feature – the tax advantages.

FOR SALE
Angelo Place
24, Onslow Street
South Perth

17 Exclusive apartments
River Views
features include:
- *New Kitchen & Bathroom*
- *Built in Robes • Light Fittings*
- *New Carpets & Window Treatments*
- *Individual Laundries*
- *Spacious Balconies & Courtyards*

An old block of 17 units, fully renovated and strata titled. Structured for wealth creation and sold in record time.

O'Rourke (09) 341 6611
O'ROURKE REALTY INVESTMENTS
62 Scarborough Beach Road, Scarborough Western Australia 6019

128 Hensman Street, South Perth

- Security complex comprising six 2-bedroom units.
- Block completely refurbished, including new façade, new electronic gates and security intercoms. Beautifully presented.
- All units sold to investors.
- Six new property managements and one strata management to our firm.

FOR SALE

Coolinda Court
128 Hensman Street
South Perth

3 Ground Floor Courtyard Apartments
3 First Floor Balcony Apartments

Prime Residential Location
features include:
- *New Kitchen & Bathroom*
- *Built in Robes & Light Fittings*
- *New Carpets & Window Treatments*
- *Individual Laundries*
- *Huge Private Courtyards & Balconies*

O'Rourke
O'ROURKE REALT
62 Scarborough Beach Road, Sca

Old block of 6 two bedroom units, completely gutted and restored like new. Sold all six to investors.

24 Lansdowne Road, Jolimont

- Security complex comprising twelve units – four 1-bedroom and eight 2-bedroom.
- Totally refurbished throughout, both interior and exterior, including new façade, new carports, storeroom and roof. From a very ordinary looking block of flats, the complex came up a treat.
- All twelve units sold, most through our investment seminars.
- Property managements on most of the units to our firm.

Sold all 12 to investors before the brochure was printed.

24 Lansdown Road, Jolimont

64 Gardner Street, Como

- A block of eight units – four 2-bedroom and four 1-bedroom.
- Fully revamped.
- Five units sold to one client who needed tax minimisation.
- Six new property managements to our firm.

Como

From $125,000
64 Gardner Street
8 Refurbished units
From $7 a day you can own a second property
Basic requirements
• currently a wage earner
• ample equity in your own home or great city residence

O'Rourke
O'Rourke Realty Investments

The big draw from this advertisement was –
From $7 a day you can own a second property. One client bought five for investment from this advertisement.

FOR SALE

64 Gardner Street, Como

4 Security Apartments with Leafy Courtyards
4 Security Apartments with Spacious Balconies

Marketing is all about packaging

NEGATIVE GEARING EXERCISE

Marketing Plan for 64 Gardner Street, Como

		1 BRM UNIT	2 BRM UNIT	1&2 BRM UNITS	
PURCHASE PRICE		120,000	145,000	265,000	
FIRST MORTGAGE (90%)		108,000	130,500	238,500	
EQUITY REQUIRED 10%		12,000	14,500	26,500	
1 X 1 Bed					
1st MORTGAGE @ 6.95%	108000	7,506			
1 X 2 Bed					
1st MORTGAGE @ 6.95%	130500		9,070		
1 X 1 & 1 X 2 Bed					
1st MORTGAGE @ 6.95%	238500			16,576	
Less rental Income					
Unfurnished 50 Weeks a Year		7,000	8,000	15,000	
Less 25% Outgoings		1,750	2,000	3,750	
Nett Rental		5,250	6,000	11,250	
SHORTFALL PER ANNUM		2,256	3,070	5,326	

Each client's tax bracket is effected by not only his or her earnings, but also by the amount of deductions. The following figures are the amounts the client actually pays out of his own pocket after taking away the Rental Return and the Tax Rebate.

Could you afford $7 per day for that extra investment property?

373–5 Cambridge Street, Wembley

A quite recent listing is for a block of sixteen fully refurbished units. I had spent three years talking to the owner of this development, advising him over that time. During the four months that the property was being gutted and refurbished, we had a large display sign at the front. It promised all those who inquired in response to the sign that they would be invited to a preview showing before the units were advertised to the public. This generated more than a hundred inquiries. You have to be prepared to do the public relations; it will pay off 90 per cent of the time.

On the opening day, we had at the site Bob Lomas of Able Finance, who represents about thirty banks. We sold one unit in the first hour for the full asking price of $154,950, and went away from the showing with several hot prospects.

FOR SALE

WEMBLEY   **FR. $139,950**

*REFURBISHED APARTMENTS IN THE
HEART OF WEMBLEY!*

- *CHOICE OF FIRST FLOOR OR GROUND FLOOR*
  - *FRONT & REAR COURTYARDS*
    - *SECURITY PARKING*
    - *EVERYTHING LIKE NEW*
  - *SOME UNDERCOVER PARKING*
- *UPSTAIRS UNITS WITH DRYERS*

*FOR FURTHER DETAILS:
CALL
RORY O'ROURKE
0418 903 259
or at the office on: 9341 6611*

373-375, Cambridge Street, Wembley, block of 16 units built in 1963. The son of the original owner restored them to their former glory.

SHELBOURNE
373-375 CAMBRIDGE STREET WEMBLEY

EXAMPLE ONE: 20% DEPOSIT

	2 UNITS	3 UNITS	4 UNITS
PURCHASE PRICE (@140,000 PER FIRST FLOOR UNIT)	280 000	420 000	560 000
FIRST MORTGAGE (80%) To Avoid Mortgage Insurance	224 000	336 000	448 000
EQUITY REQUIRED (20%)	56 000	84 000	112 000
2 UNITS			
FIRST MORTGAGE 224,000 @ 5.8% Int only	12 992		
3 UNITS			
FIRST MORTGAGE 336,000 @ 5.8% Int only		19 488	
4 UNITS			
FIRST MORTGAGE 448,000 @ 5.8% Int only			25 984
LESS RENTAL INCOME PER ANNUM	15 360	23 040	30 720
(160.00 PER WEEK PER UNIT X 48 WEEKS)			
SHORTFALL PER ANNUM/POSITIVE/NEGATIVE	2368	3552	4736
LESS 30% RENT EXPENSES	4 608	6 912	9 216
NET SHORTFALL PRIOR TO TAX DEDUCTIONS	-2 240	-3 360	-4 480

If you are in the high tax bracket consider buying 4 units.

SHELBOURNE
373-375 CAMBRIDGE STREET WEMBLEY

EXAMPLE TWO: NIL DEPOSIT

	2 UNITS	3 UNITS	4 UNITS	
PURCHASE PRICE (@150,000 PER GROUND FLOOR UNIT)	300 000	450 000	600 000	
FIRST MORTGAGE (80%) (To Avoid Mortgage Insurance)	40 000	60 000	80 000	
EQUITY REQUIRED Nil, Done by Equity Borrowing Against Own Home				
2 UNITS				
FIRST MORTGAGE 300,000 @ 5.8%	17 400			
3 UNITS				
FIRST MORTGAGE 450,000 @ 5.8%		26 100		
4 UNITS				
FIRST MORTGAGE 600,000 @ 5.8%			34 800	
LESS RENTAL INCOME PER ANNUM	14 400	21 600	28 800	
(150.00 PER WEEK PER UNIT X 48 WEEKS)				
SHORTFALL PER ANNUM	-3 000	-4 500	-6 000	
UTILISING ADDITIONAL SECURITY LESS 30% RENT AS EXPEN	4 320	6 264	8 640	
	-7 320	-10 764	-14 640	
EXAMPLE THREE: PRE PAY INTEREST 12 MONTHS IN ADVANCE				
ON ACQUISITION 29/6 WE WOULD HAVE THE DEDUCTION AS SHOWN EXAMPLE THREE				
	17 400	26 100	34 800	
LESS ONE DAYS RENTALS AT 30/6	42	63	84	
	-$17 378	-$26 037	-$34 716	DEDUCTION
NOT INCLUDING A % OF BORROWING COSTS				

> Better still if you were to settle in June this year, you can pre-pay the interest 12 months in advance. You would have a further deduction in the current year's tax of $34,013. Make sure you get the commercial consideration of 0.10%.

24–26 Ostend Road, Scarborough

These units were built by a major national builder for Town & Country Building Society. Another agent had had the units for sale for a period of three months without making a sale, whereas we sold the six units in eighteen hours. How was it done?

Copy of advertisement

Nine Houses Sold to One Client

A client had a house in Mount Lawley and two rental properties. He had an income of $60,000 and positive rental on the two properties, so he was paying huge tax plus provisional tax as applicable at the time. To buy the six units, he borrowed against the rental units he owned. What he borrowed was sufficient to cover:

- the six deposits
- the establishment costs
- the costs of the window treatments
- an extra $42,856 to cover the shortfall (refer to example)

We budgeted fifty weeks a year rent on all units. He still owned his own home outright, so there was potential there for additional borrowings if needed. The net result was that he reduced his taxable income through negative gearing and created accommodation for six more families, while we gained six more property managements.

With no deposit you can buy...

Units		
	1/26 Ostend Rd, Scarborough	$ 79,000
	2/26 Ostend Rd, Scarborough	$ 79,000
	3/26 Ostend Rd, Scarborough	$ 79,000
	1/28 Ostend Rd, Scarborough	$ 79,000
	2/28 Ostend Rd, Scarborough	$ 79,000
	3/28 Ostend Rd, Scarborough	$ 79,000
		$474,000

By way of first registered mortgage over property owned

	Value		Mortgage	
8/10 Regent St. West, Mt Lawley	$ 53,000		$ 45,000	
12/12 Regent St. West, Mt Lawley	$ 53,000		$ 45,000	
1/26 Ostend Rd, Scarborough	$ 79,000		$ 71,000	
2/26 Ostend Rd, Scarborough	$ 79,000		$ 71,000	
3/26 Ostend Rd, Scarborough	$ 79,000		$ 71,000	
1/28 Ostend Rd, Scarborough	$ 79,000		$ 71,000	
2/28 Ostend Rd, Scarborough	$ 79,000		$ 71,000	
3/28 Ostend Rd, Scarborough	$ 79,000	$580,000	$ 71,000	$516,000

All funds to be supplied by Town & Country

Including

Deposits	$7,900 x 6	$47,400	
Establishment costs	$3,000 x 6	$18,000	
Window Treatments	$1,500 x 6	$ 9,000	
Buffer		$13,600	$90,000

$516,000 x 16% p.a.	$82,656	
+ Annual Expenses		
Scarborough Units $2,100 x 6	$12,600	
Mt Lawley Units $1,800 x 2	$ 3,600	$98,856

LESS INCOME

Scarborough, 150 x 6 x 50	$45,000	
Mt. Lawley, 110 x 2 x 50	$11,000	$56,000
		($42,856)

Client with $60,000 income per year

By purchasing 6 x 3 bedroom units shows loss	$42,856	
+4% depreciation on buildings only, ie each building worth $50,000 excluding land and chattels		
50,000 x 4% x 6 units	$12,000	$54,856

Taxable income	$60,000
Plus net income on Mt. Lawley	$ 7,000
	$67,700

Tax on $67,700 =	$26,053	
New tax on	$60,000	
Less	$54,856	
	$ 5,144	

> He got his provisional tax back from last year. Did this help towards the following year? How much cash did he need? NONE.

No tax on $5,100 So tax at 24% of $44 = $ 10.56

$26,042.44 REFUND

Within three months this same client purchased another triplex (i.e. three homes on the one strata title) at 43 Dover Road, Scarborough, for $237,000, and once again our firm received the management of these properties.

His own home continued to go up in value. His two rental units in Mount Lawley went up. His six homes in Ostend Road went up and his three homes in Dover Road also went up.

Summing up, this client wasn't even in the market to buy real estate, but he needed to reduce his tax. What better way is there to do this while picking up capital growth as well? Naturally, more sales came into our office and more property managements.

10 March 2002 – Today I have just listed No. 2/43 Dover Road for $229,950. He had paid $237,000 for the three. **Real estate goes up**.

303 Harborne Street, Glendalough – 'Raimar Gardens' 110 Sales

The year was 1980, and this was a big one. The development consisted of 164 2-bedroom units, of which three different agencies had jointly sold 54 over a period of 2½ years. I sold the remaining 110 units over six months.

How did I go about it? The units had been numbered 1–164. The 54 units that had been sold were the ones with the lowest numbers (i.e. unit addresses), which should have given a strong clue to everyone involved. Imagine offering for sale a unit with 164/303 Harborne Street as its address and expecting people to get excited.

My key marketing proposal was to give the development an additional street number. This was done, and number 305 was created. So far so good. Then the remaining 94 units, which had been numbered 70–164, suddenly became known as:

    A BLOCK – A1-A30, 305 Harborne Street

    B BLOCK – B1-B30, 305 Harborne Street

    C BLOCK – C1-C34, 305 Harborne Street

From a marketing point of view this sounded much better. As these remaining 94 units had never been offered – they had been held back until the first two blocks were sold – we were able to offer them as 'first time offered' properties. This certainly helped as well.

Raimar Gardens, 303 Harborne Street, Glendalough

Fully Furnished
Two Bedroom Strata Title
HOME UNITS

Raimar Gardens
GLENDALOUGH

MAL DEMPSEY & ASSOC.
REAL ESTATE & BUSINESS AGENTS

Herdsman Lake Concept Plan
Metropolitan Regional Planning Authority.

Raimar Gardens, 303 Harborne Street, Glendalough

Raimar Gardens
GLENDALOUGH

Two storey. Double brick & tile. Ground floor and first floor units.

Spacious two bedroom, fully furnished units are set in landscaped gardens. Own carports and close to all amenities. Fully reticulated from own bore.

INCLUDED IN EACH UNIT
Brand new carpets, window treatments, light fittings lounge suite
5 piece Dining Suite
Bedroom 1: Double Bed
             Dressing Table and Built in Robe.
Bedroom 2: Single Bed
             Dressing Table and Built in Robe

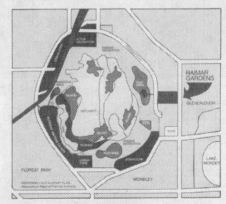

The Herdsman Lake Concept is presently being developed
to create the finest wetland habitat for
wildlife in an Australian city.

FURTHER INFORMATION CONTACT:
Jim Christie or Rory O'Rourke

MAL DEMPSEY & ASSOC.
95 Scarborough Bch. Rd.
Scarborough, 6019
Phone: (09) 341 6611 A/H (09) 447 3870

MEMBER OF R.E.W.A. & M.L.S. Licensee. M. DEMPSEY J.P.

305 Harborne Street, Glendalough

	2 UNITS	3 UNITS	4 UNITS	5 UNITS
PURCHASE PRICE (@ $25,000 per unit)	50,000	75,000	100,000	125,000
First Mortgage (80%)	40,000	60,000	80,000	100,000
Equity Required (20%)	10,000	15,000	20,000	25,000
2 UNITS First Mortgage $40,000 @ 17.75%	7,100			
3 UNITS First Mortgage $60,000 @ 17.75%		10,650		
4 UNITS First Mortgage $80,000 @ 17.75%			14,200	
5 UNITS First Mortgage $100,000 @ 17.75%				17,750
Less Rental Income Per Annum ($48.00 per week per unit)	4,992	7,488	9,984	12,480
SHORTFALL PER ANNUM	2,108	3,162	4,216	5,270

Internal shots of display unit,
305 Harborne Street, Glendalough
after being refurbished.

How Did We Get This Listing?

Why should two family companies, which had developed thousands of units over the previous thirty years, honour one firm with an exclusive agency?

Stoneham Court, corner of Powell and Stoneham Streets, Joondanna

For one thing, I was able to show the vendors a successful development I was currently marketing to add to the credibility of my proposal. This was a complex of twelve 2-bedroom units on the corner of Stoneham and Powell Streets, Joondanna – much smaller, but still relevant. As well, I had a well-considered marketing approach to present to them. Apart from the renumbering exercise, it involved:

- Creating display units that showed the full potential of the apartments. Like all the units, these were newly painted throughout and had new carpets, curtains and light fittings installed, but they were furnished to a high standard. (Needless to say, the asking price for these particular units was set higher.)

- Finding a way around the very high and very unattractive interest rates that prevailed at the time – 15 per cent. What about vendor's terms? Knowing the vendors had very large equity and had already sold 54 units – thus eradicating their mortgages – I proposed they carry finance at 13.5 per cent 'interest only' for three years to 80 per cent of purchase price. They hedged initially, but I was able to show them they were currently netting no more than about 6 per cent on the value of their investment.

- Marketing the units interstate – it was agreed I would market them throughout New South Wales and Victoria as well as Western Australia. This was done through the print media in each state. The vendors agreed to pay for the marketing costs in the two eastern states.

An Attractive Proposition

Two factors made this an especially attractive proposition to purchasers.

- Borrowing costs were dramatically reduced, the only up-front cost being stamp duty on the mortgage. There were no establishment fees, no procurement fees, no valuation fees and no mortgage insurance.

- As an offer was submitted and accepted, the vendor also approved the finance, and settlement could take place within seven to twenty-one days. So we knew that as soon as an offer was accepted the deal was unconditional.

D. E. WOOD A.A.S.A.
PUBLIC ACCOUNTANT

1st FLOOR
87 LIVERPOOL STREET
SYDNEY 2000

TELEPHONES: 264 5988
267 3178

Public Accountant D.E. Wood's Endorsement

January 21, 1982.

Mr. Rory J. O'Rourke,
Room 652,
Wentworth Hotel,
SYDNEY N.S.W. 2000

Dear Rory,

I was very pleased to meet you again on Wednesday and I well remember my first introduction to you and Mal Dempsey in Sydney in September 1980.

At that time I was naturally hesitant in investing in home units in Perth - see what you are buying and be close enough to what you have bought to keep an eye on it are reasonable maxims for real estate investment.

However, I am very glad to say that I can make the following comments about the investment I made in 3 x 2 bedroom units in Raimar Gardens, Glendalough.

My wife and I jointly own two of the units and my daughter who is a schoolteacher jointly owns the third unit with me.

There has been five weeks of vacancy in the combined three units since November 1, 1980. We have received completely satisfactory rent statements each month accounting for rents received from each unit and all expenses incurred, together with the cheque.

Whenever I have made phone calls to Mal Dempsey & Associates I have always found courteous and obliging service in regard to any queries I have made.

The tax department has accepted the taxable deductions in respect to the investments for the year ending June 30, 1981.

Finally, my wife and I have confirmed confidence in our association with you and Mal to invest in a fourth unit you have recommended to us in Scarborough.

Yours sincerely,

D.E. WOOD

With vendor's terms available the situation was that, instead of looking for people with $22,000 to buy a unit outright, we were now seeking purchasers with equity in their home or $4,400 deposit – and possibly even less, depending on their credentials. A minimum deposit of 20 per cent was normal at the time, as a bank loan of more than 80 per cent involved mortgage insurance. But in this case we had flexibility because the loans were to be on vendor's terms. If a client was an excellent risk I would suggest 90 per cent finance – a deposit of only $2,200. As a later part of this story will show, I was prepared to go even beyond this with my recommendations.

Marketing Tools

We prepared a two-colour four-page pamphlet and colour pictures of the inside of both the display units and the 'as is' units. The latter still had the original furniture, which was about five or six years old. It's amazing how different the display units looked with plants, brassware, pictures etc.

The situation can be compared with the new-home display centres. When you compare the display home with your eventual project home, it's hard to believe they are the same. It's the elaborate landscaping outside and the lavish treatments inside that change the appearance completely.

Multilisting

In the interest of the vendors, we suggested we multilist the units on the basis of one block at a time, C Block 1–34 being the first. It was fascinating to note that only one of the entire 110 units was sold by a conjuncting agent. That agent was Wayne Howes, now a partner in Townsend Howes Linney Real Estate in the Perth suburb of Morley.

I had told Martinovich and Rainoldi the biggest problem they would have would be keeping up with our sales. They scoffed at this in a good-natured way, and we all laughed. But they took it seriously enough to get right on with refurbishing the units. The fact that they were initially all occupied by tenants made it hard.

Analysis by Spreadsheet and Marketing Presentation

I prepared spreadsheets on the basis of no deposit and deposits of various figures along with different scenarios for the purchase of one through to four units.

The following steps applied to the marketing of 303 and 305 Harborne Street, Glendalough.

1. Preparing creative four-page brochure and colour pictorial showing internal views of display units versus the ordinary units.

2. Preparing summary letter showing tax advantages etc.

3. Coordinating the overall revamp and making sure the display units were ready prior to spending money on marketing.

4. Designing advertisements that would work.

5. Making sure staff, and especially receptionists and telephonists, were fully aware of what was being marketed.

6. Drafting mortgage documents as a standard template, covering full details including 13½ per cent interest, three-year term, interest only.

7. Making sure our management services were geared up to handling this sort of volume.

8. Preparing computer spreadsheets that showed how little it cost clients out of their own pockets after the tax deductions.

9. Activating the whole program.

The first advertisement appeared in the *Sydney Morning Herald* on 11 June 1980, and all 110 units were sold within six months.

On the first day the advertisement appeared, Mr Brian Stanley of the Sydney suburb of Manly agreed to buy four of the units. His accountant, Mr Peter Hunt, organised a local Perth agent – a friend of his, Mr Frank Carmichael – to inspect the units on Mr Stanley's behalf. He recommended them as good value, and the transaction took place by means of telegrams and the mailing back and forth of the entire documentation. Settlement took place within four weeks.

We received a huge number of inquiries as the weeks rolled on. I would make particular note of inquiries from accountants and solicitors, knowing their potential to persuade their clients to invest in suitable real estate.

I took a chance telephone call on the last day of July 1980 from an accountant in a very rich rural area of New South Wales, indicating he and his partner could be interested in buying one or more of the units. We arranged to meet on Saturday, 2 August 1980 at the display unit.

At our meeting I immediately went into asking them if they paid too much tax and if they were looking to buy for tax purposes. I went into considerable depth on the subject. They said I was the first real estate agent who had ever brought up the subject of taxation and negative gearing with them – after all they were the accountants, not me. Anyway, they felt it was refreshing for them to meet a real estate agent coming from this direction.

We spoke at length, and they talked of possibly buying one unit. I asked whether they would be interested if I could get them eight units using the same deposit. They laughed and said they were going to see some other agents while in Perth for the weekend. Prior to leaving Perth, one of the accountants phoned back to ask if I could really get them into eight units for $1,650 deposit in total. What I was talking about was $250 deposit on the display unit and $200 on each of the other seven. My only problem was that I hadn't put this to the vendors.

I had to move in with one of my hardest sales pitches ever. Not only were the suggested deposits tiny, at $200 and $250 they were much smaller than the commission the vendors would have to pay us for making the sales. As this amounted to about $1,000, they would have to find about $800 for each of the eight units before they began to receive any return.

My main point was that if the accountants went home and told their clients they bought eight units in Perth, the effect would be tremendous. (It would be none of the clients' business that they had purchased them on such low deposits.) After much deliberation the vendors agreed.

So we sold eight units instead of one as follows:

4 August 1980   C6/305 Harborne Street, Glendalough
                        Price $22,500 – Deposit $250

4 August 1980   C8/305 Harborne Street, Glendalough
                        Price $21,700 – Deposit $200

4 August 1980   C12/305 Harborne Street, Glendalough
                        Price $21,700 – Deposit $200

4 August 1980   C15/305 Harborne Street, Glendalough
                        Price $21,700 – Deposit $200

4 August 1980   C16/305 Harborne Street, Glendalough
                        Price $21,700 – Deposit $200

4 August 1980   C18/305 Harborne Street, Glendalough
                        Price $20,700 – Deposit $200

4 August 1980   C23/305 Harborne Street, Glendalough
                        Price $20,700 – Deposit $200

4 August 1980   C24/305 Harborne Street, Glendalough
                        Price $20,700 – Deposit $200

The accountants had hardly landed back in their town when our phone began ringing with more and more of their clients wanting to buy.

I and my principal at the time, Mal Dempsey, flew over to this particular town to talk to prospective purchasers. We spoke to dozens of people who had contacted us direct as

DAWSON & PARTNERS

Jindalee House, 92 Cooper St., Cootamundra
P.O. Box 201, Cootamundra N.S.W. 2590
Telephone : (069) 421711

Chartered Accountants

Associated with Duesbury, Johnston & Marks
Chartered Accountants
Offices throughout Australia

5 August, 1980.

Mal Dempsey & Associates,
95 Scarborough Beach Road,
SCARBOROUGH, W. AUST. 6019

> "Eight sales in one day"

For the attention of Mr. Rory O'Rourke

Dear Sir,

Nandi Holdings (Cootamundra) Pty. Limited & Kandeha (Holdings)
Pty. Limited trading as Princely Pads

Thank you for the time you spent with us over the weekend.

We confirm our purchase of Units C6, C8, C12, C15, C16, C18, C23 and C24, 305 Harbourne Street, Glendalough in accordance with the Vendor's terms as detailed on the sale advice notices.

We note that you will instruct the Vendor's Solicitors to prepare the appropriate contracts and send them to us in the near future.

We also confirm that the Companies will be joint purchasers as Tenants in Common. Both Companies are incorporated in New South Wales and have their Registered Offices at 92 Cooper Street, Cootamundra.

The Directors of Nandi Holdings (Cootamundra) Pty. Limited are Hazel Mary Sullivan and John Clifford Sullivan. The Secretary is John Clifford Sullivan and Contracts will be signed by Hazel Mary Sullivan as Director and John Clifford Sullivan as Secretary.

The Directors of Kandeha (Holdings) Pty. Limited are Annette Patricia Bilton and Robert Ian Bilton. The Secretary is Robert Ian Bilton and Contracts will be signed by Annette Patricia Bilton as Director and Robert Ian Bilton as Secretary.

Should you require Directors' Guarantees we have no objection to that.

We will be discussing the matter of the block at Scarborough Beach with a Client in the next few days and we will then be in touch with you again.

Yours faithfully,
DAWSON & PARTNERS

Partners: J. C. Sullivan, B.Ec., A.C.A.,   R. I. Bilton, B.Comm., A.C.A., A.L.G.A.

well as to clients of the accounting practice. The result was selling the entire 110 units – as I say, in a period of six months.

One family to whom the accountants had introduced to me bought eighteen of the units on the one day. This is the deal I have already mentioned. We were told this was a new Australian record for number of individual sales sold in one day through the multilisting service. **My first multi-listing record of 18 sales in one day.**

Why did one New South Wales family buy eighteen 2-bedroom units in Glendalough, Western Australia?

- They could buy three units in Perth for every one in Sydney.
- Did they really buy eighteen units? They only put 10 per cent deposit on each unit, the vendor carrying the rest.
- With the same amount of money they could have bought only 1.8 units outright.
- They needed tax deductibility.

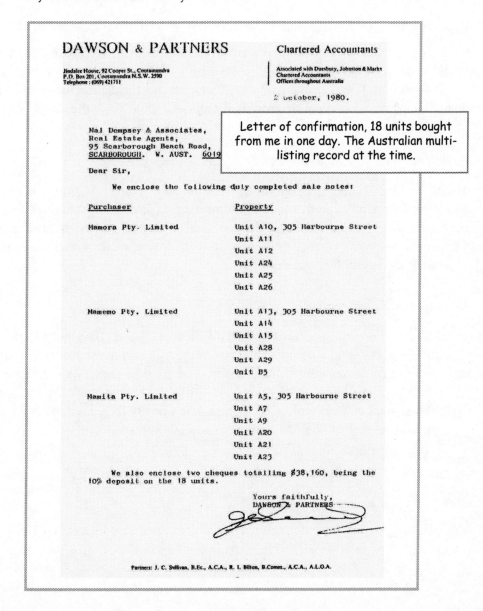

DAWSON & PARTNERS

Jindalee House, 92 Cooper St., Cootamundra
P.O. Box 201, Cootamundra N.S.W. 2590
Telephone : (069) 421711

Chartered Accountants

Associated with Duesbury, Johnston & Marks
Chartered Accountants
Offices throughout Australia

2 October, 1980.

Mal Dempsey & Associates,
Real Estate Agents,
95 Scarborough Beach Road,
SCARBOROUGH. W. AUST. 6019

Dear Sir,

> Letter of confirmation, 18 units bought from me in one day. The Australian multi-listing record at the time.

We enclose the following duly completed sale notes:

Purchaser	Property
Mamora Pty. Limited	Unit A10, 305 Harbourne Street
	Unit A11
	Unit A12
	Unit A24
	Unit A25
	Unit A26
Mamemo Pty. Limited	Unit A13, 305 Harbourne Street
	Unit A14
	Unit A15
	Unit A28
	Unit A29
	Unit B5
Namita Pty. Limited	Unit A5, 305 Harbourne Street
	Unit A7
	Unit A9
	Unit A20
	Unit A21
	Unit A23

We also enclose two cheques totalling $38,160, being the 10% deposit on the 18 units.

Yours faithfully,
DAWSON & PARTNERS

Partners: J. C. Sullivan, B.Ec., A.C.A., R. I. Bilton, B.Comm., A.C.A., A.L.O.A.

Their taxable income was approximately $100,000. By buying eighteen units, each on 10 per cent deposit, the net result was a tax loss of $42,000; i.e. rental income less all expenses including all the interest repayments showed a negative gearing result of $42,000. Their taxable income now looked like this:

Taxable income	$100,000
Less negative gearing	$ 42,000
New taxable income	$ 58,000

What they saved in tax paid half of their total input, including the deposit.

Over the years each of these units has grown in value from an average of $22,000 on purchase day to $50,000 in 1988 to today's price of $80,000. That's an increase of $58,000 per unit. What's that as a return? Remember that the deposit was only $2,200 on each unit. We need to put the estimated profit of $58,000 over the initial deposit:

$$\frac{\$58,000}{\$ 2,200} = 2636.36 \text{ per cent or } 125.54 \text{ per cent p.a.}$$

The purchase worked so successfully that the same family bought the Burrendah House Shopping Centre in Willeton, a southern suburb, the following year and three shops in the Heathridge Shopping Centre, in the north-western corridor of Perth, the following year. The accountants themselves over the next two years bought a total of seventeen properties, all on very nominal deposits.

How's your own marketing going?

My Australian multilisting records of 1980 I believe still stand today, i.e. 18 sales in a day, 36 in a week, 48 in a month, 123 listed properties sold in the one year and 110 sales in the one year, the last two figures actually achieved within a six-month period. How could you possibly do these volumes by listing and selling houses on the normal basis? These were only my multilisting figures – they do not include all my other sales. That same year I bought into Mal Dempsey and Associates.

I sold some 600 Perth properties to New South Wales clients from 1980 to 2001. Approximately 250 properties were sold to people in the same town alone.

How's that for marketing?

Marketing New Strata Title Villas and Townhouses

- Sold on behalf of Austmark Group
- 68 units in 4½ months
- Location – Scarborough and Doubleview
- New units built on spec, all sold on the basis of possible future growth and the tax benefits, in that order

Unit Development
Doubleview

133 Deanmore Road, Scarborough

A few years later we were selling one of these at 133 Deanmore Road, Scarborough, and the adjoining neighbour dropped in and said, 'Just having a sticky-beak'. When I suggested he buy it, he said he was pushing to pay his current debts. I asked if he would buy if I could show him how he could afford it. He looked at me blankly. I followed it up the next day and qualified him properly. His financial structuring was completely incorrect.

1. He had a seven-year principal-and-interest loan on his unit. Trying to both pay off the principal and cover the interest was killing them.

2. He was paying off a hire-purchase loan on a courier van to a major finance company at 25 per cent (principal and interest again) with $25,000 outstanding.

3. He owed $17,000 on a second vehicle, paying principal and interest through another finance company at 23.5 per cent.

4. They had three or four credit cards, having started with one.

The picture was getting worse. Let's analyse this situation:

1. Mortgage on home:

   > $36,000 principal and interest
   >
   > 7 years at 15 per cent
   >
   > Repayments per calendar month $695

2. Courier vehicle:

   > $25,000 principal and interest
   >
   > 5 years at 25 per cent
   >
   > Repayments per calendar month $734

3. Second vehicle:

   > $17,000 principal and interest
   >
   > 5 years at 23.5 per cent
   >
   > Repayments per calendar month $484

4. Credit cards

   > $10,000
   >
   > Monthly payments approx. $200

Thus their debt was $88,000 and their monthly repayments were:

(1)	695
(2)	734 (tax deductible)
(3)	484
(4)	<u>200</u>
	$2,113

They were both working, and wondered why they were not getting anywhere. Remember, we must always look at the tax situation. To pay (1), (3) and (4), the non-deductible items, they needed to earn say 30 per cent more to cover tax. Therefore to cover their repayments of $2,113 per month, or $25,356 per annum, they would have to earn $30,850 gross annually over and above their everyday living expenses and the costs associated with running the courier vehicle.

If we restructured the borrowings as follows, they would be able to buy the unit next door and their outgoings would be less.

Refinance existing unit, worth $130,000, to 90 per cent of value = $117,000.

$117,000 interest-only loan at 15 per cent = $1,462.50 per calendar month or $17,550 per annum.

New refinance	117,000
Less total debts	88,000
	$29,000

No cash deposit required to:

Buy extra unit	125,000
15% deposit	19,000
	106,000

$106,000 at 15 per cent interest only = $1,325 per calendar month or $15,900 per annum.

Rental at $140 per week x 52 weeks	7,280
Less rates and taxes	1,000
Managed by themselves	0
	$6,280
Interest paid on new unit	15,900
Less net income	6,280
	9,620
Plus interest on new borrowings on existing home	17,550
	$27,170

Compare this to previously paying $30,850. It was an actual saving of $3,680, and they now have two properties appreciating. They had also reduced their tax.

All monies borrowed for investment purposes are tax deductible. *Let me say it again: this applies even to money borrowed on your own home. It is not where you borrowed the money; it is why you borrowed the money.*

From the $29,000 surplus borrowed we used:

Mortgage insurance	2,500
Deposit on new unit	19,000
Establishment cost	4,000
	25,500
That left a buffer of	3,500
	$29,000

As I have explained, the buffer is the security blanket. I encouraged them to put the additional saving of $3,680 into the same buffer as well as the tax savings.

The $9620 shortfall on the second property is tax deductible, as are the borrowing costs (the proportion of the new equity borrowings obtained to buy the extra unit). Let's say that in the first year their taxable income was reduced by $11,000. With a tax rate of 30 per cent, they would see a further benefit of $3,300. That's real money.

And they now have two properties going up in value.

Property One	130,000
Property Two	125,000
	255,000
If capital growth was 10% p.a. first year	25,500
	280,500
Capital growth second year (10%)	28,050
	$308,550

Based on their expenses in the past, do you think they would have ever saved $25,500 in a year, let alone $28,050? What do you think the capital growth on the cars was? There's no argument about that: they go down in value. What risk did they take? The client asked, 'What if I want to get out of my courier vehicle'? My reply was, 'You own it outright!'

Surely 15 per cent interest is better than the 23.5 per cent and 25 per cent they were paying on the vehicles. Interest rates now are much cheaper, but a similar comparison can still be made. It's amazing how many people I come across with huge equity in their homes, yet they have expensive second mortgages, hire purchase, leases, personal loans and numerous credit cards. Why don't they restructure?

What did I get out of this deal? A sale! That's creative marketing.

Luxury Apartments

Take the example of Blue Bay Apartments in Mandurah, south of Perth. We sold fourteen of them in 1982 while the local agents sold two.

The units were priced from $125,000 up to $220,000. Returning to an old theme, I ask this question: How many people today carry around $125,000 in their wallet? Not many. Do they really need that amount of money to buy one of these properties? Haven't we heard of mortgages? How much money do they really need? None, if they have equity in their own home. Why do we persist in advertising the purchase price? There is a lot to be said for advertising investment properties without any mention of a figure – low deposit/no deposit subject to conditions.

Blue Bay apartments, Valley Road, Halls Head, Mandurah.

Let's look at a deposit of 20 per cent and work on the cheapest unit. $125,000 now reads $25,000 deposit. But who said they have to find even that amount? That is the lender saying they would like to restrict the deposit to that figure so they don't have to get involved in arranging mortgage insurance. Doesn't the developer want the units sold? Then why isn't he helping? What's to stop him leaving 10 per cent in as a second mortgage?

He is now receiving 90 per cent of the purchase price and leaving a bit of his profit in the development. If he isn't satisfied with the security, why should the purchaser feel confident in paying the asking price?

He agreed to leave 10 per cent in, which meant I was now looking for people with $12,500 through to $22,000 deposit for the dearest unit. Did every one of our purchasers take up the second mortgage? No. But we certainly took these units from a minority market through to a majority market.

This points up the advantage of having an investment analyst. In our case, having that position has improved profitability in all divisions. It is by far the best way to lift profits, and it generates income all the time. Working in conjunction with our Property Management and Sales Division, it has become the dominant factor in our overall profitability.

BLUE BAY - MANDURAH

	1 SUITE (UNIT 2)	2 SUITES (11 & 20)	3 SUITES (8, 12&15)
PURCHASE PRICE	126,000	303,000	433,500
First Mortgage 75%	100,800	242,400	346,800
Equity Required (Nil using your other properties as collateral security)			
Borrow full purchase price plus $10,000 per unit it cover establishment costs.			
One Suite			
First Mortgage 136,000 @ 17.75%	24,140		
Two Suites			
First Mortgage 323,000 @ 17.75%		57,333	
Three Suites			
First Mortgage 463,500 @ 17.75%			82,271
Less Rental Income (Minimum Guarantee for 1 Year Period)	6,552	15,756	22,516
SHORTFALL PER ANNUM	17,588	41,577	59,755

With interest rates of 17.75% at that time. Negative gearing was still justified, paying 17.75% interest is better than your tax rate.

BLUE BAY - MANDURAH cont'd

Each client's tax bracket is effected by not only his or her earnings, but also by the amount of deductions.
The following figures are the amounts the Client actually pays out of his own pocket after taking away the
Rental Return and the Tax Rebate.

TAX BRACKET					17,588	41,577		59,755
To 17,894	30.67c in $				12,194	28,825		41,428
To 34,788	46c in $				9,498	22,452		32,268
Above 34,788	60c in $				7,035	16,630		23,902

Capital Gains are calculated over a five year period for the property purchase value. The following is
calculated on a flat rate appreciation of 10%.

NO. OF SUITES:		1ST YEAR	2ND YEAR	3RD YEAR	4TH YEAR	5TH YEAR
One	126,000	138,600	152,460	167,706	184,476	202,923
Two	303,000	333,300	366,600	403,260	443,586	487,944
Three	433,500	476,850	524,535	576,988	634,686	698,754

It must be remembered, the return will improve as rent increases.

Remember the interest on money borrowed for investment purposes is tax deductible.

Vacant Land

Ants don't pay rent. **Who helps you pay for vacant land? No-one.**

A normal house takes up approximately 30 per cent of the land it sits on. Who pays for the rest? If I am going to buy a 1,000 m² block I want a triplex or a quadruplex on it, giving me three to four times the return of a single house. This is the reason why, with residential real estate, I generally recommend home units rather than houses. As I have pointed out, another very good income-producing real-estate investment is strata-titled commercial units.

An example, in the residential sector, is 27 Drabble Road, Scarborough. The original house, on a 1,800 m² block, was returning $160 per week rent. Six townhouses have now been built behind the original home, and all seven properties are rented for approximately $150 per week each, making for a total of $150 x 7 = $1,050 per week.

Is this an improvement?

"Creative thinking"

1-7/27 Drabble Road, Scarborough

Often young people buy vacant land because their parents and grandparents purchased land originally, and then built on it once they owned it outright. Because land is so expensive today, it is usually necessary to borrow a large amount as a mortgage – besides having to pay shire and water rates and land tax. This does not make for an attractive proposition.

With clients who want to make their first move into real estate, it is better to advise them to buy income-producing property such as a strata-titled unit. This is a stepping-stone to eventually owning their own home. It can be negative geared, so two other parties are helping to pay for the property – the tax department as well as the tenant – while at the same time the property is picking up capital growth. Down the track the client can buy a second and maybe a third investment property.

When they want to build, they can sell a couple of investments, buy that dream block and build immediately. The capital growth across the two or three investment properties will be far greater than that on the one block of land they might have bought, and the tenants and the tax department have paid most of the bills.

I give the same advice to established developers and first-time developers: buy vacant land only if you are going to develop immediately. The holding costs can be horrific. Don't buy on the basis of anticipated zoning changes – no-one knows what the future holds. I have known people with a duplex site in an area where there were only a few such blocks. They were holding off, waiting for sewerage to come through that area because the zoning would change from R20 to say R30. But as this happens to their site, it also happens to 90 per cent of the other sites, and suddenly they are all triplex blocks. The value will not necessarily become greater. It all has to do with the law of supply and demand.

Eastern States Trip Paid Dividends
Multiple Sales – 22 Sales in One Day, 6 February 1982

My best day of sales

16/133 Deanmore Road, Scarborough	$51,000	Page
4/52 Sackville Terrace, Scarborough	$31,000	Partlett
3/52 Sackville Terrace, Scarborough	$31,000	Partlett
2/55 Deanmore Road, Scarborough	$26,000	McAuley
4/133 Deanmore Road, Scarborough	$51,000	Partlett
2/133 Deanmore Road, Scarborough	$51,000	McAuley
1-8/10 Dover Road, Scarborough	$364,000	Rimosa Pty Ltd
1-8/15 Dover Road, Scarborough	$372,000	Rimosa Pty Ltd

It was certainly one of my better days in real estate when I sold twenty-two units to one family. I had booked two adjoining apartments in the Wentworth Hotel in Sydney in 1982, setting up one unit as our office and the one adjoining as our accommodation.

I was fortunate in meeting Mr Ron Stiles, a lovely fellow who had sold out his cabinet works to a public company. He was impressed by what we were recommending in Perth, but said he needed to see the properties. Within a week of our return he and one of his daughters arrived in Perth.

The twenty-two units they purchased comprised eight strata-titled units at 10–12 Dover Road, Scarborough, for $364,000, another block of eight units at 15–17 Dover Road for $372,000 plus six individual strata-titled units in Deanmore Road and Sackville Terrace, Scarborough.

Twenty-two sales in one day to one family. This meant twenty-two new property managements to our firm.

133 Deanmore Road, Scarborough

52 Sackville Terrace, Scarborough

10 Dover Road, Scarborough

15 Dover Road, Scarborough

On another day I sold **eleven** 2-bedroom villas to a brother and sister, Peter Allen and Kath McKeown, who were painting contractors. They purchased five villas at 249 St.Brigids Terrace and six at 42–44 Brighton Road, both in Scarborough.

They each had a house to live in. Why did they buy eleven more properties? It was to reduce their tax and increase their wealth. Could you be any better off? How much money do you need? None – if you have sufficient equity in your own home. And the same applies to your clients.

42–44 Brighton Road, Scarborough

249 St Brigids Terrace, Scarborough

5 Brentham Street, Leederville, Western Australia

Block of twenty-two 3-bedroom home units approximately 3 kilometres from the centre of Perth, built in approximately 1991.

We had sold 16 of the units, and I suggested to the developer to keep the remaining six units. Mr and Mrs Ricciardello, the developers, were wanting the funds for their next project. I suggested that his profit had to be somewhere in the last six units, which he agreed was correct, although he refused to tell me how much!

I suggested that they should borrow against the equity in the last six units, based on the sale price of the other sixteen to 80% of the value. This would free up 80% of the value. Did they have to pay tax on the sum they took out? No, and as he borrowed the funds for investment purposes the interest was tax deductible.

After lengthy discussions, they did what I recommended. We sold two of the remaining units eight years later, nine years later and eleven years later at times when it suited them to taxwise.

The latest two we sold recently for $195,000 and $197,000 each were tired looking.

Creative Tax Planning

We had the developers spend say approximately $10,000 on each, which was maintenance, and tax deductible. So it really cost the developers $5000 as it was tax deductible.

If the new purchasers had bought the units and spent $10,000 on carpets, verticals, new tiling and painting, it would be called capital improvements and not tax deductible. The same cost of $10,000 would have really cost them $20,000 as it was after tax money they were spending.

From a Rental Perspective:

These units were now like new, so we got a better rent of perhaps $30 per week. The higher the rent , the better class of tenant is achieved, and the tenants are responsible for keeping the units in the same condition as when they rented them.

If the property is grotty, and a tenant takes it, that is generally how they live, and the property will generally be worse when they move out.

From the developers point of view, the units increased in value from 1991 to 2002, and they were receiving rents for the eleven years.

We got the property management and strata management fees for the same period.

FOR SALE

LEEDERVILLE $199,950

CHOICE OF TWO FANTASTIC TOWNHOUSES!

- 3 LARGE BEDROOMS
- 2 WCs
- FULLY REFURBISHED INTERIORS
- CHOICE OF STREET FRONTAGE OR PARK VIEWS
- SEPARATE LOUNGE
- 2 CAR BAYS
- CLOSE TO CAFÉ STRIPS & CITY

FOR AN INSPECTION CALL RORY O'ROURKE
MOBILE: 0418 903 259   OFFICE: 9341 6611
www.orourke.com.au

SOLD
PERTH REAL ESTATE GUIDE

5 Brentham Street, Leederville

The Ricciardello's built another block of eight units at 44 Calais Road, Scarborough shortly afterwards, and kept the entire eight for about nine years.

We once again handled the Property Management and the Strata Management.

Over the years we have sold hundreds of properties for the Ricciardello family through creative marketing.

21

Public Private Partnerships/ the Private Finance Initiative

I am happy to share with you information about a new development that is about to change the whole picture of public real estate ownership in Australia. It is one that presents us with another opportunity, as real estate agents, to become leaders, not followers.

We have spent two years studying the changes that have been taking place in Britain under the banner of 'Public Private Partnerships' (PPP) and the 'Private Finance Initiative' (PFI). In pursuing this, we have brought to Australia one of Britain's experts on these subjects, Mr David Lane, (twice, the latest February 2002) in order to get a first-hand grasp on this revolution in public infrastructure provision. As guests of David Lane, we have also gone to Britain, Ireland, France and Wales to look at how the system works there.

Fifty different countries are currently looking at the British success story. The governments of New South Wales, Victoria and Tasmania have recently released a green paper on the new approach, and the Western Australian government will be releasing a paper by July 2002.

Public Private Partnerships have come about as a result of the British Government accepting that there will not be sufficient taxation revenue to pay for the facilities needed by government institutions. The outcome is that the Government supplies the private sector with the land and very precise documentation on the 'services' they require, while the private sector provides the building and undertakes to maintain it.

There is no cost to the Government until handover, following completion of the building. The Government then remits a monthly payment covering rental and maintenance. The maintenance fee is calculated over twenty-five years and averaged to a monthly figure. The land and the building revert back to the Government after twenty-five years.

The schemes go beyond provision of buildings, as will be explained. The main thing to be noted is that this is not private enterprise *per se*; rather it is a partnership between the public and the private sectors.

Best Value for Money

The private sector generally has a better track record in management of property, and this is an important element in the success of the new approach. But the biggest factor is capital cost savings. If the Government does not have to outlay the cost of constructing these buildings, this makes available more money for enhancements such as:

Police	More police on the beat
	More money for information technology
	Better equipment
	More presence generally
Health	New hospitals
	Upgrading of existing hospitals
	Upgrading of equipment
	Better conditions for staff
	Better conditions for patients
	Better information technology
Education	Better and higher education for staff
	Better conditions for staff
	Better conditions for students
	Better equipment
	Better designed facilities

Every project is designed, built, financed and operated by the private company/consortium. In the past too many of these institutional buildings were poorly designed. For example if a school was required for four hundred students, they would construct twenty classrooms, each to accommodate twenty students. Today classrooms in British schools are purpose-built according to the subjects that will be taught in them – whether that be information technology, science, manual arts etc. – and also the ages and stages of the students.

In old schools, maintenance bills can be so horrific that the buildings simply have to be replaced. Once a school is built under the new scheme, the Government does not need to worry about maintenance, which is taken care of under the PPP arrangements.

Here is an example of how PPP works.

Expressions of interest are called for a new school – or say for ten new schools in a region. A consortium wishing to bid for the project will consist of an operations manager, facility operator, builder and banker. Tenders are called on the basis of design, build, finance and operate (DBFO). A short list of consortia is determined, and finally the winning consortium is selected.

A new school is built on the playing fields adjoining the old building, after which the latter is demolished and the grounds redeveloped to a specified standard. The PPP contract will incorporate maintenance of the building and grounds for say twenty-five years. It might also involve the supply of all furnishings and fittings. If heating or airconditioning is specified, the suppliers have to warrant the system for the twenty-five years. Do you think they will put in the best equipment or the run-of-the mill variety? Large penalties are payable in the event of any failure in performance.

The cost savings through this system have proved to be huge, largely due to the immense efficiency of the private sector. Without having to outlay millions of pounds on buildings, the British Government has more money to put into other elements of the infrastructure.

I have been working with David Lane for the last two years. We have made submissions to the previous West Australian Liberal Government and are now awaiting an invitation to engage in discussions with the current Labor Government.

How Are These Schemes Financed?

Why would the Bank of Scotland provide finance through the Private Finance Initiative?

- Freehold title to the land.
- Government-guaranteed tenant for twenty-five years.
- Bank releases money on a progress draw basis – cost to complete. They only advance monies as work is completed, always holding back enough to complete the project.

How do the consortia make a profit? By efficiency and careful budgeting. In the best case, they might well recoup their outlay by the twenty-first year. As well, they have first right to renew the maintenance contract at the end of the twenty-five-year term.

This is not unlike state governments selling off many of their state housing homes to the private sector. Why are they doing this? They are bad investments. In some states the average rent on such a home might be $76 per week, yet the maintenance could be more than $5,000 a year or say $100 per week.

Government is involved in no capital outlay and no maintenance expenses if the private sector supplies the same unit of accommodation. If the property is positively geared, the Federal Government receives tax on the profits and tax on the capital gains. If it is negatively geared, the Government loses a small amount in tax revenue but hopes to accrue capital gains tax in the longer term. No government in the world can house its people, and negative gearing is one of the best initiatives taken on behalf of any government. The alternative in Australia – the Government having to supply accommodation for the ageing population – is frightening.

From an investor's point of view, why should the banks get all the better deals? What is our biggest worry with investments generally? They are the vacancy factor and maintenance. Imagine a new police station in your town. Why wouldn't you buy it if you had guaranteed rent for twenty-five years and the consortium guaranteed the maintenance?

We see ourselves as facilities managers. This role is of equal and growing importance as compared with that of the facilities provider. We see ourselves and our clients owning these types of projects in partnership with government. Beyond this, we see ourselves participating in projects outside the realm of real estate, for example as operators of special purpose vehicle (SPV) fleets. With David Lane as our expert associate, we see ourselves acting as advisers to governments, banks, builders, engineers and managers of projects set up under the Public Finance Initiative and Public Private Partnership. It's a whole new world. We see ourselves as being leaders in this new field, as we are at least two years ahead of anyone else.

This is the best opportunity real estate agents have ever had. It will lead to the creation of complete new departments within our industry, as that industry is turned upside down. Why wait until you have missed another opportunity? Remember, 'Knowledge is Power'.

The Fundamentals of Public Private Partnerships (PPP)

This approach – federal, state and local governments partnering with the private sector with the aim of gaining best value for both taxpayers and government – is increasing in importance as a method of service provision and procurement. We are positive that it will be of interest to the Australian state governments, which all have low taxation on their political agendas.

The following are insights provided by our PFI and PPP expert, Mr David Lane.

The Private Finance Initiative (PFI) was announced by the UK Chancellor of the Exchequer in the autumn of 1992.

The purpose of PFI is to enable government and other public bodies to contract with private sector companies/consortia on a design, build, finance and operate (DBFO) basis for infrastructure and other projects Under PFI, the public sector

Rory (centre) pictured with David Lane (right) – Rory making omelettes for 20, with three eggs! South Africa, 1985. David is now our PFI expert, 2002.

provides the core services (such as medical healthcare in a hospital or teaching in a school) and the private sector provides the non-core (support) services.

The public sector defines its non-core service requirements in terms of 'Output Service Specifications'. A process of competitive tendering then enables the private sector to propose the most cost effective and efficient way of achieving these requirements, frequently including an element of income generation.

PFI contracts extend significantly beyond, but do include, the provision of new buildings. The range of support services provided might include:

- Maintenance and repair
- Catering
- Cleaning
- Laundry
- Energy
- Information technology
- Maintenance of equipment (including vehicles)

Private sector funding and operating of facilities that have been traditionally provided by the public sector is intended to enable the expansion of investment in public facilities without a related increase in government/public borrowing.

The UK Government requires acceptable PFI proposals to offer:

Value for Money

PFI can allow higher quality, more expensive buildings to be supplied at reduced annual cost to the Government.

Annual costs (to the Government) are worked out as an average over the life of a project. It is in the interests of the private sector to fund and build high-quality buildings in order to gain long-term savings, for example in terms of maintenance. These potential savings also mean that the public sector bodies can benefit not only from lower annual costs (than could be achieved through government funding) but also from long-term guaranteed costs, giving them the ability to plan ahead with certainty.

Transfer of Risk

PFI is designed to transfer significant risks to the private sector. The risk transfer covers each stage of a DBFO contract, and might include for example:

- Design hindering effective service delivery
- Construction costs overrunning
- Losses through completion delays
- Escalating lifecycle repair/service provision costs
- Inability to meet income-generation scheme target

Off Balance Sheet

The finance structure of an acceptable PFI proposal must comply with relevant accounting rules to ensure that the project is regarded as 'off the public sector balance sheet'.

PFI Sectors

Within the UK, PFI is currently being applied to the following types of projects:

Air traffic control

Building refurbishment

Electronic re-engineering

Global telecoms

Hospital and health facilities

IS/IT infrastructure

Magistrate's courts

Office accommodation

Police stations

Power and energy

Prisons

Radio communications

Railways

Roads

Schools, colleges and universities

Staff accommodation

Student accommodation

Underground transportation

Vehicles

Waste management

Water and sewerage

All sections of public procurement are included.

A more detailed account by David Lane of the new system follows overleaf:

The Story of PFI and PPP

David Lane offers a more extended account of the Private Finance Initiative and Public Private Partnerships.

Introduction

The Private Finance Initiative was launched in 1992 by the then Conservative Government to open up opportunities for more private sector involvement in the provision of public services. The thinking behind this initiative was and remains that the public sector will procure the services to quality standards that it defines *rather than* procuring a capital asset or equipment and then operating it itself. It is a requirement that the private sector delivers the service using a capital asset or equipment that it owns for the contract period, and is thus responsible for its maintenance.

One of the benefits for government in procuring services this way is that the 'risks' are placed with the partner best able and experienced to handle them. For example, the risks associated with owning, designing, constructing and maintaining a capital asset are all risks that the private sector companies are used to dealing with and are therefore best placed to manage. Successful delivery of partnership projects offers good value for money for the taxpayer against the traditional procurement method. The level of payment by the public sector is based on the performance of the private sector operator against agreed and defined levels of service.

The incoming Government of 1997, far from discarding the procurement regime of the previous administration, has enhanced and strengthened it. Under the global banner of 'Public Private Partnerships', PFI has become one of the main mechanisms through which the public sector can achieve the improvements in value for money the Government seeks.

The underlying difference between previous procurement methods and this new approach is the need to be serious about the 'partnership' element of the process. Without a commitment to partnership from both sectors it would be extremely difficult to effect a successful PFI contract.

Scope

It is anticipated that PFI can and will be used in all fields of public procurement for the foreseeable future. Encompassed in this are IT, education, prisons, health, transport, government buildings, police, ambulance and fire services and defence.

Education

- the provision of new school buildings coupled with the disposal of any redundant ones
- the provision of university student accommodation
- the provision of modern and practical teaching and research facilities
- the provision of state-of-the-art IT systems

Health

- the provision of new and refurbished hospitals coupled with disposal of any redundant ones
- the provision of nursing accommodation

Transport

- the provision of new roads
- the provision of bridges and tunnels
- the provision of light rail systems

Police

- the provision of police buildings coupled with the disposal of redundant ones
- the provision of state-of-the-art IT systems
- combining operation resources with fire and ambulance services
- the provision of helicopters

Defence

- the provision of training facilities such as flight simulators
- the refurbishment of housing estates

Successes

Since 1997 (in Britain) contracts using the PFI procurement method have been signed to the value of some £12 billion, covering 150 projects drawn from all public sectors:

- 35 major hospital projects
- 520 schools and 4 prisons
- 28 defence contracts
- projects to modernise the government estate

The Government estimates that savings already achieved from signed contracts amount to some £2 billion when compared to the traditional method of procurement. This represents a 17 per cent saving, equivalent to 25 new hospitals or 130 new schools.

Future

A stated commitment recognises that the public and private sectors have distinctive but complementary parts to play in achieving the objectives of modernising the country's infrastructure and service provision through some combination of each sector working together in partnership. The record so far shows that the public services now being supplied not only meet the required standards but are of better quality and at demonstrated best value.

The savings currently being made through such partnership arrangements are tangible, are meeting the needs of customers and provide for and protect the wider public interest.

An official announcement confirms that spending on schools in England and Wales to the period ending April 2003 will be in the order of £1.65 billion. Other government departments will have similarly planned expenditures – especially transport, where many new road systems have been announced.

Combining the public and private sectors in partnership ensures that the required public services will be supplied far earlier than the traditional procurement would have allowed. Furthermore, long-term maintenance is planned into the life of any contract, ensuring the quality of the service provision from a public sector perspective.

Many UK services are conducted out of old buildings, sometimes poorly placed to deliver quality service and sometimes not easily adapted to modern service activities. PFI allows a mechanism whereby some of these problems can be overcome.

Addressing Questions Often Raised About PFI

PFI projects are often complex, involving the Government and the supplier adopting innovative approaches, and this often prompts questions about the policy. This section addresses the questions most frequently raised.

Why does PFI offer value for money when the private sector's cost of borrowing is higher than that of the public sector?

First, it is important to put this into perspective. The difference between the private sector's cost of borrowing and that of the public sector is down to some 1 to 3 per cent[1] and this additional margin applies only to a relatively small proportion of the total cost of each PFI contract – capital expenditure forms on average just 22 per cent of the total cost of PFI projects.[1]

---

[1] Value for Money Drivers in the Private Finance Initiative, Arthur Andersen and Enterprise LSC (2000)

Second, and as a result, the value extracted from the use of the funds raised is normally more important than the price paid for them. The private sector can compensate for the higher price of its borrowing in a number of ways:

- It can be more innovative in design, construction, maintenance and operation over the life of the contract.

- It can create greater efficiencies and synergies between design and operation.

- It can invest in the quality of the asset to improve long-term maintenance and operating costs.

- Underlying all this, the discipline of the marketplace ensures the private sector can manage risk better – it has better incentives and is better equipped to deliver on time and within budget. As the Institute of Civil Engineers and the Faculty and Institute of Actuaries in their publication on risk management state, 'The Private Finance Initiative has heightened awareness of project risks in ways that traditional procurement has hitherto not been able to do, so that the identification, allocation and management of risks have grown to become essential parts of the PFI process'.[2]

Third, in reaching a judgement on whether a PFI contract will offer value for money, and therefore whether to proceed, the Government compares the contract with an assessment of the cost of alternative public sector financing and management – the Public Sector Comparator (PSC).

In July 1999 the Government commissioned Arthur Andersen and Enterprise LSE to carry out a study of 'Value for Money Drivers in the Private Finance Initiative'. The report was published in January 2000, and submitted as evidence to the Treasury Select Committee. It confirmed that PFI is delivering better value for money, and indicated that PFI projects are on average delivering savings of 17 per cent over traditional forms of procurement.

Some examples of the better value obtained by PFI include the following:

- In the National Savings contract signed in January 1999 for the transfer of business operations, the PSC indicated that the traditional procurement option would be over 20 per cent more expensive.

- The Falkirk school PFI deals are estimated to offer 15 per cent better value for money.

- Defence projects average between 10 and 15 per cent better value and in some cases up to 20 per cent (for example, the project to train crew for the Medium Support Helicopter).

---

[2] Risk Analysis and Management of Projects, Thomas Telford Publishing (1997)

- Prisons averaged 10 per cent better value for initial deals signed under the previous Government and an average 13 per cent (assuming optimal public sector risk management) to 18 per cent better value (assuming good public sector risk management) for recent contracts.
- The first four DBFO road projects are likely to deliver savings of around £100 million (10 per cent).

Is value for money achieved by exploiting staff?

No. The terms of employment for staff transferred to private sector management are protected under TUPE in the vast majority of cases. In addition, the Government has announced measures to protect pension entitlements. Staff recruited by contractors benefit from the Government's general reforms of employment legislation covering issues such as pay and working hours.

Why not just relax the rules on public borrowing to allow more investment by public sector bodies?

The Government announced, in the 1998 Comprehensive Spending Review, a £10 billion increase in public sector investment over the following three years, consistent with its fiscal rules. The Government's approach is to use PFI where it would provide better value for money compared to public sector investment, as described above.

Doesn't PFI just mortgage the future?

PFI requires properly considered decisions about long-term service delivery requirements. The financial commitments entered into during the life of the contract provide not only a physical asset but a guaranteed service to specified performance levels.

Under a conventionally procured project, the public sector would still have to meet the cost of maintaining the asset and providing the service. In the past, capital has often been invested without a clear commitment to adequate spending on maintenance, leading to poorly maintained assets, high running costs, inefficient service provision and premature replacement. In contrast, PFI invests in the future because it ensures that assets are maintained properly and can revert to the public sector at the end of the contractual period in good condition. This amounts to sound budgetary planning.

It is also worth noting that long-term PFI contracts often contain break points or options at the halfway point, and at regular periods thereafter, to give the public sector flexibility over the service that is being delivered by the private sector party. Some National Health Service contracts are an example of this.

To make them affordable, don't PFI schemes lead to small facilities and reduced levels of public service?

It is sometimes suggested, particularly in the context of health projects, that PFI schemes are not affordable unless they are made smaller in size and scope than the facilities they replace, for example by reducing bed numbers in new PFI hospitals. However, the affordability ceiling and the level and mix of services to be delivered under any new capital investment project are determined long before the private sector is involved in negotiations.

To use the National Health Service as an example, the services to be provided at any new hospital – which in turn determine the number of beds needed to deliver them – are set out in an initial 'Outline Business Case' (OBC). This is drawn up by NHS managers, clinicians and health experts and must be approved by the Department of Health before a decision is taken on whether to use public capital or the PFI route to fund the project. An affordability ceiling must also be determined for the OBC and, together with the number of beds required, must be included in the first tender documents that go out to prospective private sector bidders under the PFI route.

The reductions in bed numbers at new hospitals have been driven by developments in medical techniques and practices such as the increased use of day surgery and shorter hospital stays. It is not a result of the introduction of PFI.

What is wrong with traditional public procurement?

There is a history of conventional projects that have overspent their original budget, or which have been delayed. Some examples include:

Trident Submarine Shiplift and Berth (Pasiane, Scotland)

- initial cost estimate £100 million, final cost £314 million
- total slippage in completion date – 2½ years

Jubilee Line Extension

- initial cost estimate £2.1 billion, final cost some £3.5 billion
- total slippage in completion date – almost 2 years

The New En-Route Air Traffic Control Centre

- total initial cost estimate £475 million, latest estimate £655 million
- total slippage in completion date – 5 years

Guy's Hospital

- initial cost estimate £36 million, final cost £160 million
- total slippage in completion date – more than 3 years

22

Learning from Mistakes and Moving Forward

Since 1962, when I started my first job, I have had a hiccup every seven to nine years. Remember, I am Irish and God didn't give me a brain. I sometimes think I've made more mistakes than anyone I've ever met – but I most certainly learn from them.

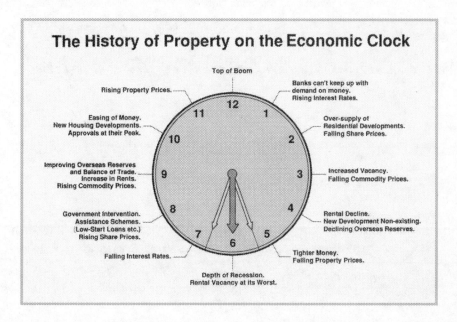

My big setback started in 1988 compounding by1992, when the Keating recession was taking its toll on a lot of entrepreneurs. I was already staggering when the ATO hit me with a huge bill for provisional tax. You remember the system: we hadn't even earned the money yet, and they wanted the tax in advance *plus* a 12 per cent surcharge.

Australian Taxation Office
1 St George's Terrace, Perth 6000

Income Tax Assessment Act 1936

NOTICE OF ASSESSMENT
for the year ended 30 June 1988   (or substituted accounting period)

Your file number

Make sure that you show
this number on all
letters and your next
income tax return form

Issue date

21 FEB 90

273684/013
DR = Debit CR = Credit

MR RORY JAMES O'ROURKE
C/O WINDUSS & COOK PTY
PO BOX 100
SCARBOROUGH 6019

Details of your assessment:

```
YOUR TAXABLE INCOME IS $120783                        $      C
TAX ON TAXABLE INCOME                          A   52034.67DR
MEDICARE LEVY                                  O    1509.78DR
PROVISIONAL TAX ON 1988 INCOME + 12.0% (NOTE 4) B  60827.00DR
ADDITIONAL TAX FOR LATE RETURN (NOTE 6)        C   14415.81DR
CREDIT FOR 1988 PROVISIONAL TAX                F    1966.00CR
BALANCE OF THIS ASSESSMENT                     L  126821.26DR
THIS AMOUNT IS PAYABLE BY 26 MAR 90
```

This was my provisional, my
wife paid a similar figure.

A bit rough when I only
earned $120,783.

```
********************************          TION *******************

ADDITIONAL TAX FOR LATE RETURN CALCULATED A
ADDITIONAL  5% PA FOR THE  2ND RECURRING O

KEEP THIS NOTICE!  YOU WILL NEED IT TO OBTAIN INFORMATION
ABOUT YOUR PERSONAL TAX AFFAIRS FROM THE TAXATION OFFICE.
```

NAT97-10.88

B.F. POWER
Deputy Commissioner of Taxation

Your copy — please keep for your records
back for notes and other information

R2
Total amount payable $ 126821.26

Date due and payable   26 MAR 90

Australian Taxation Office

Notice of Instalment of Provisional Tax

Income year ending 30 June 19   90

	File number
MR RORY JAMES O'ROURKE C/O WINDUSS & COOK PTY PO BOX 100 SCARBOROUGH 6019	**Issue date** 21 FEB 90
Provisional tax amount (*see Note 2*)	$60827
Instalment number	1, 2 & 3
Instalment amount IN TOTAL	44085.00DR
Reduction of previous instalments (*see Note 3*)	0.00
Income tax outstanding/credits	0.00
Other instalment amounts outstanding/credits	0.00
Amount payable/refundable	44085.00DR
Date due and payable (*see Note 4*)	26 MAR 90

```
     THIS IS A COMBINED NOTICE OF INSTALMENT OF PROVISIONAL
TAX FOR INSTALMENTS 1, 2 AND 3. THE AMOUNT PAYABLE FOR EACH
INSTALMENT IS      $14695 .
```

273684/013

B.F. POWER
Deputy Commissioner of Taxation

Your copy — Please keep for your records

NAT 1350–7.89

There had been a day when you paid tax on what you had actually earned. There had also been a day, if memory serves, when banks would try to see their clients through difficult patches. I can't say mine did anything wrong, strictly speaking. But a little bit of flexibility on its part could have made a big difference at the time. As a matter of fact one of the senior managers who handled our account said as much to me recently, and I take a little consolation from that. Rory, he said, if we'd kept you afloat for another six months, you'd still be worth millions.

Little did he know. **I'm back, worth millions.**

But let's go back to the beginning. Mum and Dad sent me to a convent school, Our Lady of Grace in the Perth suburb of North Beach, upon our arrival from Ireland. Have you ever met a rich nun? Rich in other ways no doubt, but not in worldly goods. After a year at Our Lady of Grace I went to CBC Leederville. Have you ever met a rich Christian Brother? They had to give up their assets to gain the cloth. Whilst I have the utmost respect for all my ex-teachers what could either the nuns or the Christian Brothers teach us about money management? This was hardly their speciality!

In the school system they taught me that the smart people in this world are accountants, schoolteachers, solicitors and bank managers. I have met very few rich individuals from those professions. What were their biggest mistakes? If you've been following the argument of this book you'll know the answer: paying too much tax and not borrowing enough money.

I tried numerous endeavours in the early days while still developing and playing with real estate. These included:

1960 Commenced a band-booking agency called 'Mr Gassers Enterprises'.

1962 Commenced work with a building company while studying cost accounting.

1963 Ran cabarets, battles of the bands and river cruises, still under the name of 'Mr Gassers Enterprises'.

1964 Opened a nightclub in partnership – 'Mr Gassers Place' in Wellington Street, Perth.

1966 Joined North City Holden, under the banner of Automotive Holdings, working in the Costing Department (while still studying accounting).

1968 Transferred to sales – the best sales experience you can get (selling cars).

1968 Bought my first home, at 66 Odin Road, Innaloo.

1969 Got married. Bought second home, at 11 Giles Street, Trigg.

1970 Received many awards and prizes for sales and marketing in the car business. Bought third home, at 25 Giles Street, Trigg.

1972 Set up the Roadside Group of Companies with two others from North City Holden.

1973 Bought a block of shops on the corner of Newcastle Street and Charles Street, Perth. I opened Erins Antiques and set up the first YMCA Adult Education course in antiques.

1974 Started Homestead Real Estate Pty Ltd and Homestead Developments Pty Ltd, both operating from 103 Flora Terrace, North Beach. We undertook dozens of developments during the next five years as well as selling lots of properties.

1976 Bought next home, at 13 Muller Street, Trigg.

1979 Bought our current home 9 Belhus Drive, Trigg.

As I've indicated here, I started work as a costing clerk while studying accountancy. Why didn't I complete my accounting qualification? I kept visualising myself back in the roaring twenties wearing a peaked cap in a back room checking invoices and counting other people's money. No, I was not that old, but I did not want to become the modern-day equivalent. Today I am in a unique position with my background of both accounting and marketing.

In 1976 I was fortunate to be introduced to the Apex Club of Hamersley by my good friend Cliff Hynam. It was through the Apex International Division of the World Organisation (WOCO) that our world changed.

Our first international relations tour representing Apex Australia took us through Singapore, Kuala Lumpur, Malacca, Seremban and Penang. When you are home-hosted, you see how other people live. As you only get to meet these people say for twenty-four hours, you must break down the barriers. One thing I would ask them was this: 'Do you own your own home?' They all laughed and said no, they were renting. In 1977 they were all renting and never expected to own a property. During the day we were in tour groups with other service club members – good interaction on a bus or plane – and would ask the same question. We would always be first to put up our hands to host overseas WOCO members.

In 1979 we were fortunate to represent Apex Australia in Scotland. We stayed with twelve families during a period of fourteen nights. During the day we were travelling around the country, and I asked our hosts and our fellow tourists, all from other service clubs throughout the world, what the situation was like in their country. Did they own their own homes? The majority answered no: that would be an impossible dream. Home ownership had long gone for them.

While in Scotland we visited Edinburgh Castle. What was the status of the people who had lived there – rich or poor? Obviously rich. Outside the castle walls, where the city now stands, had been Edinburgh village. What about the people who lived there? Rich or poor? Poor, without a doubt. You were one or the other.

In later times the middle class came into being. What distinguished members of that class? They owned their own homes. Following this line of thinking I saw that, if home ownership goes, it will leave only rich and poor, just as had been the case in Edinburgh those many years ago. If owning one's own home was no longer a possibility for the people we met in Scotland, it was going to disappear in Australia also. How could we be spared?

We went on to represent Apex Australia in seventeen countries, among them Malaysia, Singapore, England, Ireland, Scotland, France, Denmark, Sweden, Holland, Germany, Wales, New Zealand, South Africa and Belgium. Middle class is gone for future generations in most of these countries, and I saw it was quickly disappearing in Australia also.

In 1979 I spent a short period with Barrie Manners and Associates; then in April of that year I met Mr Mal Dempsey of Mal Dempsey Real Estate. It happened like this: while walking down to the beach, my wife and I saw a sign on 9 Belhus Drive, Trigg, indicating that Mal Dempsey was selling the property. She said we should buy it. We did, and twenty-three years later we are still there. Having met Mal Dempsey through making the purchase, it was not long before I joined his firm. It was in mid-1979 that I started to realise that *we needed to change how residential real estate is marketed professionally*. My attack was on the biggest expense we all have – it is tax without doubt.

One thing I became very aware of at the time was how most people complain about the interest they pay on their home mortgages. And nowadays many wait for another ¼ per cent drop in rates before buying a home. How ridiculous.

'Wealth-Building' – How We Started

In the outline of events near the beginning of this chapter there is a brief chronicle of some of my early moves into buying real estate. While most people buy a house and take out a principal-and-interest loan over twenty to thirty years, even that brief summary will have shown how I approached things a little differently right from the start.

First came the purchase of 66 Odin Road, Innaloo, in 1968 for $11,950. I put down $2,950 as deposit, took out a mortgage for the balance and let it for $30 a week. Over the next few years I carried out renovations, spending $2,200 and supplying my own labour.

In 1969 we had the property revalued and then refinanced it in order to buy the first of three properties we ended up purchasing in Giles Street, Trigg. No. 11 cost us $12,950, of which we paid $3,000 as deposit, and again we rented it out for $30 a week.

When Robyn and I married earlier in 1969, we initially lived in a granny flat attached to my parents' home at 36 Mary Street, Waterman, though I already owned 66 Odin Road. What helped us at the time was that the rent we paid was much less than the amount we were receiving for our own place. Late in the following year, 1970, we moved into the Odin Road house and continued renovations.

In 1970 the opportunity came up to purchase 25 Giles Street, and we made an offer. We had no sooner done this than the City of Stirling condemned the house! But the location justified the purchase, and we knew what we wanted to do with the property, so we went ahead. When we bought them, nos. 11, 25 and (later) 19 were the worst houses in Giles Street, but it was an excellent street with panoramic ocean views, and we didn't doubt that we were investing well.

We sold Odin Road in 1972 and moved into 11 Giles Street, which by this time we had completely renovated, outlaying $8,050 in the process. We were on the move again in 1976, when we purchased 13 Muller Street, also in Trigg, and onsold Giles Street.

Meanwhile, in 1973, we had refinanced the two houses in Giles Street and purchased Lot 124 Padbury Circle in Sorrento, another northern Perth suburb, which was a large duplex site overlooking a sunken park. It also had panoramic ocean views.

In the following year we refinanced once again and acquired 19 Giles Street.

When we purchased 9 Belhus Drive in 1979, we sold 13 Muller Street and moved into the new place. This was our third move in Trigg, and like the others it involved a shift of only about 100 metres. But this time we stayed. Every property you ever owned and sold never went up in value again – or did it? Yes it did. So why did you sell it?

Before
9 Belhus Drive, Trigg

The neighbours think we are cheapskates. We never needed to hire a removal van, but simply wheeled the furniture along the road.

We paid $48,000 in 1979 for our current home, putting down a deposit of $10,000 and borrowing $38,000 on vendor's terms. It was an old asbestos shack on a duplex site situated 150 metres from the Indian Ocean with panoramic views to Rottnest Island and up to Hillarys Marina. We overlook the only two-street frontage house along the entire coast.

We do not hear the noise from West Coast Drive, yet we still have the beautiful sounds of the ocean. Yachts, windsurfers, fishing boats and Rottnest ferries are regular sights. We have the ocean breezes as well as all the other pluses.

We'd had the choice of going inland and buying a 4-bedroom, 2-bathroom home for the same money, but we chose *position*. In 1981 we started restoration on the outside, internal improvements having commenced on day one. The ceilings had been held up by timber uprights, which were dangerous, so we pulled them (the ceilings) down, lined beneath the roof tiles with pine and used metal brackets to readjust the roof structure. The kitchen was replaced and the exterior was brick veneered. We also excavated under the house, which was up on timber stilts, to create a huge games room that also had ocean views.

After
9 Belhus Drive, Trigg

To the east of our home we built a second one, a 3-bedroom, 1-bathroom duplex using the equity in the land. By using the equity for capital improvements, we were able to borrow the money to do the external renovations on our place while also financing the duplex. We had the luck of the Irish, because naturally we bought the only house in Australia that went up in value.

Choice: build a tennis court or build the second unit? We could have gained more friends if we had built a tennis court, but if I'd asked them to pay to play they wouldn't be friends any more.

Have you ever wanted to pick and choose your neighbours? You can do that by owning the property next door. So we built the unit and have rented it out now for twenty years.

Our original debt was $38,000. The two properties are now worth about $1,500,000. Two years ago we paid the $38,000 off and then borrowed an equity facility. With our equity facility we pay interest only on the money that is borrowed and not on the total amount of whatever the facility may be. This enables us to prepay interest and settle whatever other bills come in.

Peace of mind is important to all of us. Debt is good as long as it is on income-producing real estate.

I have mentioned meeting two accountants from a New South Wales farming community in 1980. Through that encounter I met a senior solicitor who did a lot of work with the tax office. While talking with him I said something along the lines of how unfair it was that we had to pay 60 cents in the dollar income tax. He said, 'Rory, you don't have to pay it. From what he said I created the following statements.

1. You don't have to pay tax.

2. Shouldn't we all be chasing capital wealth rather than taxable income?

3. It's not what we earn, it's what we have left after tax!

This was like me (a Catholic) meeting the Pope. I had these phrases inscribed on wooden plaques and show them to my clients each day. The best performing asset in the world is income-producing real estate. Why income-producing? Because ants don't pay rent.

The properties must have buildings on them to negative gear, and to be able to pre-pay your next years interest.

Let's analyse the tax map opposite and the properties that we had owned at different times.

Imagine if we still owned these properties:

Address	Paid	Area	Estimated worth today
11 Giles Street, North Beach	$ 12,950	506 m²	$ 825,000
19 Giles Street, North Beach	$ 14,950	506 m²	$ 825,000
25 Giles Street, North Beach	$ 9,800	503 m²	$ 820,106
13 Muller Street, North Beach	$ 38,000	506 m²	$ 825,000
281 West Coast Drive, North Beach	$148,000	506 m²	$ 825,000
293 West Coast Drive, Trigg	$310,000	761 m²	$1,240,757
9 Belhus Drive, Trigg	$ 48,000	974 m²	$1,588,000
	$581,700		$6,948,757

Hindsight is a wonderful thing! We do still own 9 and 9A Belhus Drive, Trigg, which is Lot 25 Belhus Drive near the top left corner of the map.

This story is not taking into account all the other properties we have bought and sold.

We must learn from history! If the above happened in the last 33 years, the same will more than likely happen in the next 33 years.

Rory O'Rourke

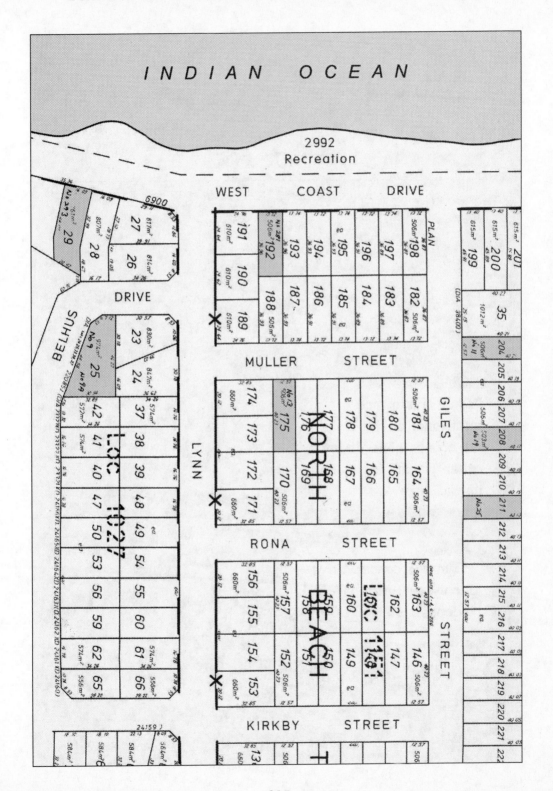

My Own Home

April 1979: Purchased $48 000
Deposit $10 000
Mortgage $38 000

1981: Increased mortgage to $90 000 ➡ Revalued after unit built $160 000
Equity $70 000   and built adjoining unit $ 90 000
    Equity $ 70 000

1983: Revalued complex $260 000
Increased mortgage $140 000
Equity $120 000

1987: Revalued complex $380 000
Increased mortgage $190 000
Equity   **$190 000**

> *Isn't this a nice additional buffer: Of course none of my other properties went up did they??

1989: Estimated market value $600 000
Mortgage $190 000
Equity $410 000

2000: Estimated market value $900 000
Less original mortgage $ 38 000
Equity   **$862 000**

> *I'm too conservative— I only put in an original deposit of $10 000

3 August 2000
Paid out first mortgage $ 38 000
Borrowed new equity facility $500 000

1 December 2001
With the sale of 10 Muller Street, North Beach at $1630 per square metre and with ours being 974 square metres this makes our property worth $1 588 043

WILL IT EVER GO UP AGAIN???

23

Communication

Communication is one of the most important aspects of business today, and good communication skills can be one of your chief assets.

For communication to take place, there have to be at least two people. It is said that God gave us one mouth and two ears, so naturally he wanted us to use them in that ratio. Even so, you may have knowledge that other people could benefit from. They cannot do so unless you have the ability to communicate it to them.

Public Speaking and Debating

An excellent place to start is public speaking and debating. I was introduced to these activities through Apex Australia, of which I was a proud member from 1976 to 1987, finishing as a District Governor and being awarded Life Membership. I have referred to other aspects of my experience with Apex in the previous chapter.

The improvement I saw in people just from joining the organisation was amazing. Some were at first shy or introverted, others suffered from stuttering, but I saw their confidence grow and with that their ability to express themselves and relate to others. Later one wondered if these were really the same people who had joined only a few years previously.

Apex began in Geelong, Victoria, as a non-denominational, non-sectarian young men's organisation, though today many clubs include women in their ranks. The age of members ranges from about eighteen to forty five. Apex is part of WOCO, a world organisation of service clubs.

I would unhesitatingly recommend membership of Apex to all young people. Of course there are other organisations, such as the Rostrum group, that encourage and promote communication skills and self-development generally.

Communicating Inside and Outside the Organisation

Communication skills are important both within an organisation and in its interactions with the world outside it – in particular its clients. Passing on our knowledge to colleagues within the firm is clearly of importance, as is establishing our credibility with clients through product knowledge. We need also to learn how to create rapport and build trust; we need to convey our credibility and trustworthiness.

We must have both clarity and assertiveness in our dealings with clients. Our brain has to be like a bucket of worms, constantly moving in different directions, especially when handling difficult people and tough situations.

A positive first impression is important, and our presentation must be polished and professional. But, just as in our personal lives and with our friendships, we need to be genuine and sincere.

Communication is the most important skill we can have – and it can be improved with practice. When you combine excellent communication skills with product knowledge, your value to any organisation is enormous.

Rory Gets Life...

Rory reaches the Apex of service

Neighbourhood News September 23 1986

Rory O'Rourke has become only the eighth member of the Hamersley Apex Club to get life membership. Life membership is not given lightly and members must have at least nine years' service. Hamersley Apex was formed more than 20 years ago and about 400 members have passed through its ranks. Among the major projects the club has been involved in are the Carine Riding for the Disabled, where 2000 hours of labour were put in by members.

Life membership for Rory O'Rourke – presenting his certificate are (from left) Lance Hammond, club president, Steve Rewell, Rory and Peter Lunt.

Restoration of the old North Beach Surf Club (now called the Apex-clubrooms) and various charity fund-raising events also have been special projects.

A recent initiative of the club has been the twice-yearly blood transfusion mobile clinic at the Apex clubrooms. The clinic was previously a joint project with Hamersley Jaycees at Aintree Hall, but due to falling numbers it was split. Response to the new clinic has than doubled from on 80 donors when it started less than 18 months ago. The club meets at the clubrooms every first and third Tuesday of the month at 6.30pm. Contact Steve Rewell on 447 5700.   ASHLEY ZANOTTI

Raising Your Profile

Raising your profile will repay you one hundred fold, over the years I have tried not to miss an opportunity.

SUNDAY TIMES, NOVEMBER 20, 1988

Land ahoy! and real estate rush rolls on

RORY O'ROURKE is something of a real estate guru — at least that is the impression after speaking with him for a few minutes.

He lectures extensively in real estate in vestment by using tax laws to advantage and will embark on a whistlestop lecture tour of three eastern States centres later this month.

His philosophy, he says. is Just common sense and has its basis in negate* gearing legislation.

He said: "We all pay too much tax. We should be chasing capital wealth rather than taxable income.

Borrowed for Investment purposes - even on your own home — is tax deductible.

I'm no longer a glorified chauffeur who drives people around the metropolitan area looking for their dream home that is yet to be built.

I'm looking for investors people who think they pay too much tax. I've never met anyone who thinks they should pay more tax.

"Before the introduction of negative gearing, people were buying for capital

Rory O'Rourke...
we all pay too much tax

growth and tax deductibility in that order of importance, but that has now been reversed.

I practise what I preach. I have 70 properties and every one of them Is going up in value.

The tenants are paying for them and the tax department is picking up the shortfall and it is fully legitimate.

Join Australia's Investment Planner of the Year 1988

Making Money Made Simple All New for 1989

featuring
Noel Whittaker

Special Session!
Practical Advice to Get You Started with Negative Gearing
featuring

Australia's Foremost
Real Estate Investment Analyst
Rory O'Rourke

Invest, not save is Rory's catchcry

A self-confessed Perth critic of banks and building societies sees investment, particularly in real estate as a means to minimise tax.

Real estate agent and tax expert Rory O'Rourke expressed the view in a keynote speech at a REIWA seminar this week.

WARNING TO ALL AGENTS
STOP LEAVING YOUR KEYS IN THE IGNITION, AS YOU PUT OUT AND PICK UP YOUR HOME OPEN SIGNS

The Sunday Times, May 20, 2001

Rory's chariot going, going, gone

Realtor Rory O'Rourke's cherished chariot should soon be back on its surfside Scarborough working patch.

The $60,000 luxury silver Statesman was nicked by a pair of brazen crooks.

Incredibly, it happened while Rory was loading his "house open" signs in the car's boot.

"I thought it was someone coming for a late home inspection but they flashed passed me and drove off" he groaned.

"I just went numb."

Rory's case has caused a buzz in real estate circles. Agents commonly leap in and out of their cars dropping off and picking up sale boards as they dart between properties.

Coppers have nicked a couple of suspects after Rory's limo was seen being stripped in a suburban driveway.

Rory, 55, a 39-year real estate veteran, has turned to his trusty ute while his favoured work wheels are reinstated to their full glory.

24

Investment Seminars on Wealth Creation

I open our weekly investment seminars by asking the audience, 'Were your parents rich?'. They all answer no. I ask why isn't there a subject in Year 10, 11 and 12 of school on finance, hire purchase, leasing and renting. Everyone agrees there should be. So why isn't there? The answer is that governments can control poor people, but cannot control the rich. Another thing I always ask is this: What is your biggest expense? I get numerous answers, but never the right one. I point out that the right answer is **tax**.

I follow this with another line of questioning. Why, as members of the middle class, do we knock the wealthy, especially when we look at the minimal taxes they pay? Instead of whingeing, shouldn't we learn how they manage to pay a smaller percentage of what they earn on tax? There are methods to legally reduce tax, so why don't we know about them? The reason is that we haven't taken the time to learn about them. We would rather complain and knock a lot of the entrepreneurs of this country.

Have the entrepreneurs created any jobs for Australians? Do those workers pay tax? The answer to both is yes. Would this add up to more tax than the entrepreneur might individually pay? Definitely *Yes!*

Dad's Assets

Then I talk about my dad. When he dies, what will his assets be? Basically they will be the same as he had fifty years earlier, i.e. one house, one car and a few dollars in the bank. Let's have a look at those assets:

I see the house as a duplicate of the original one he bought when we arrived from Ireland. It has a roof, four walls, front and back doors, a bit of glass, a hot water system and a cooker. The original house had the same.

The car, however, must be a Lear jet. Being Irish, I can't see the wings. All I see is a body, four doors, a bonnet, a boot, five bits of rubber and an engine. His original Holden cost £500. This Holden Commodore cost say $28,500. Obviously a Lear jet.

If he has double the amount in the bank when he dies, compared to the change he was left with fifty years earlier after he bought the original house and car, what is the buying power of that money now? Where have his entire working life's earnings gone? Most went in taxes.

Negative Gearing

During one of my seminars in October 1998 I asked those present (only four people – one of the smallest groups ever) if anyone could do with a tax deduction. I got a pretty positive response to that question, but no-one seemed to know the answer to the next. What limit is there on negative gearing? Of course I told them there was none. Whether you need a $2,000, $20,000 or $2,000,000 deduction, all you have to do is buy enough real estate from me. With the right structure, I said, we can eradicate the tax.

In the next few days I sold one couple a block of ten new 3-bedroom, 2-bathroom villas, a large 2-storey duplex pair and two refurbished units in South Perth. This wasn't a bad result from a seminar attended by only four people. How much money did they need? None – they owned their home outright and had excellent cash flow from their business.

What did they buy? Tax deductibility and capital wealth. Is their own home still going up in value? Yes, and the same is true of course of the other fourteen properties.

Looking at Our Mistakes

In the seminar I always put the question, 'How long are we dead for?' Most will say a long time. Then I ask, 'Do you make mistakes every day?' I don't get too many hands shooting up at that point, so I go on. Weekly? Monthly? Yearly? How about some time in the last century? Most will admit at least one mistake – they are human. What I'm trying to get them to see is that one of their big mistakes could have been not getting into negative-geared property investment.

During the seminar I show various slides. The first one shows an ostrich with its head in the sand. The final slide is of me riding an ostrich in Ooushorn, South Africa. There are a lot of other ostriches in the same pen, and I ask the audience how many of them were game to put their heads back in the sand while I remained in the pen with them.

If I can change centuries of habits of the ostriches, perhaps I can change your thinking too.

Rory rides an ostrich in South Africa in 1985

Looking to the Future

Over the years people have asked me how I can be still competing in this very tough industry after such a long time. My response is that you must be passionate, whatever industry it is that you work in. We spend more awake time in our jobs than we do with our families.

Let's live our dreams. There is nothing that we each can't achieve as long as we are willing to dream. Make your dreams reality.

I love real estate. I am not money driven. If I was, I would charge for my time. However, if money comes from what I do, I will take it every time. Guess what? The money certainly comes.

At fifty-six years of age I can't wait for the next thirty-five years in this great industry. Believe me, it will change as much in the next thirty-five years as we have seen in the last thirty-five. I get a real buzz seeing my sons equally active in the building and real estate industries.

Don't accept no for an answer. If you want something badly enough, persist until you achieve your goal.

Rory J. O'Rourke

Born Free
Taxed to Death

by Rory J. O'Rourke

Would you be any wealthier if you didn't have to pay any tax?

Also by this author, published in 2002.

Rory J. O'Rourke, real estate licensee, entrepreneur and property investor has come back from the 'financial dead' on more than one occasion. Now he is a multi-millionaire once again. Rory, in this book shares his life lessons and the secrets of how to become one of the most successful real estate salespeople in Australia.

Available on video

O'Rourke "Wealth Creation Seminars"

Taken at one of our weekly seminars on wealth creation, this video shows you how to:

Increase your wealth and reduce your tax, so you can retire early!

In the audience are some of our clients you read about in this book, Neil Darch, Charlie Kemp, Angelo and Carmel Rossi.

If you can't get to a seminar – buy the tape.

Order Form

Please send me: **Book** – I Sold 22 Homes In One Day   ___@ $35.00   A$_____.00

Book – Born Free Taxed to Death   ___@ $30.00   A$_____.00

Video – "Wealth Creation Seminar"   ___@ $55.00   A$_____.00

Total amount – *price includes GST and P&H within Australia)*   **A$_____.00**

I am paying by;   Cheque ( )   Bank Card ( )   Master Card ( )   Visa ( )

| _ _ _ _ | _ _ _ _ | _ _ _ _ | _ _ _ _ | Expires | _ _ / _ _ |

Card holder's signature _____

Name on card _____

Cheques should be made payable to **O'Rourke Publishing Pty Ltd**

62 Scarborough Beach Road, Scarborough WA 6019

Telephone: (08) 9341 6611   Facsimile: (08) 9341 6447
Website: www.orourke.com.au   **Email:** publishing@orourke.com.au

Mr/Mrs/Ms   First Name _____   Surname _____

Company Name _____

Address _____

State _____   Post code _____   Telephone _____

Email Address _____